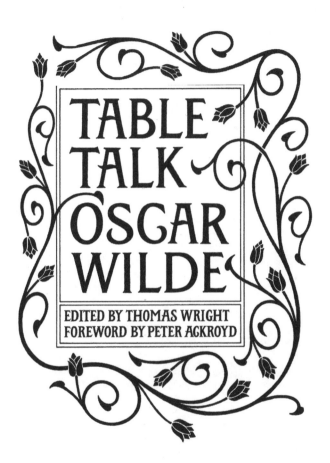

TABLE TALK OSCAR WILDE

EDITED BY THOMAS WRIGHT
FOREWORD BY PETER ACKROYD

For Mary Fanning

Special edition for Past Times

First published in the United Kingdom in 2000 by Cassell & Co,
Wellington House, 125 Strand, London, WC2R 0BB

This edition 2001

Text copyright © Thomas Wright
Design and layout copyright © Cassell & Co

A CIP catalogue record for this book is available from the British Library.
ISBN 0 304 35594 1

Publishing Director: Margaret Little
Design Director: David Rowley
Art Editor: Austin Taylor
Designer: Nigel Soper
Editors: Jamie Ambrose and Stephen Guise
Jacket artwork: Ken Wilson

Printed and bound in Great Britain

PAST TIMES®

TABLE
TALK

OSCAR
WILDE

Contents

BIBLICAL TALES

POEMS IN PROSE

Foreword by Peter Ackroyd

I T IS PLAUSIBLE TO SUGGEST that only half of Oscar Wilde's genius resides in his published works. He belongs in the company of other conversationalists, such as Johnson and Coleridge, whose wit and inventiveness were too exuberant to be confined to their written words. In the company of others, Wilde was not so much a wit in the conventional sense as a seer and magus; such was the power of his personality, in fact, that it suffuses the texts written down here from the memory of those who knew him. Even after his trial and incarceration he remained a magnificent and prolific inventor; as Mr. Wright suggests in his introduction, Wilde could no more stop telling stories than he could cease breathing. He was also an innate fabulist, continually seeking to burnish and gild the world with stories or tales which contain the sacred and the marvellous in equal proportion.

It may come as a surprise to those who know only his plays or his epigrams that Wilde had a strong and habitual sense of the spiritual. His secular as well as his biblical tales evince an awareness of damnation or redemption not untouched by irony and a recognition of the vagaries of God's grace. Yet his deity was not always or necessarily Christian. In his early childhood, he was imbued with the tales of Celtic *faerie*, and part of his power springs from his awareness of that ancient and wilful world. That is why this volume reveals the true contours of his imagination, which had its roots in Irish folklore as much as in the work of the French Symbolists or that of earlier English dramatists.

In that sense, too, Wilde helped to reintroduce the oral tradition to Victorian literature. He perfected the art of the dialogue in his critical writings, and exemplified the power of oratory in his subsequent trials. For the true melody and majesty of his voice, however, we may turn with confidence to these hitherto uncollected stories. Here lie the foundations of his unique genius.

Wilde as a young man. G. B. Shaw called him 'incomparably great as a raconteur', and the artist William Rothenstein thought him 'a unique talker and storyteller'.

Introduction

'T ALK,' DECLARED OSCAR WILDE, 'is a sort of spiritualized action, and conversation one of the loveliest of the arts.' From his days at Portora Royal School in Enniskillen, where he transformed the most banal incident of school life into a fantastic legend for his classmates, to the Parisian death-bed upon which he expired mid-sentence, Wilde scattered endless words around him – to the delight and amazement of his listeners.

One aspect of Wilde's speech is preserved in the countless collections of his witty aphorisms. In these, he sums up the world in a phrase, and all existence in an epigram. Another facet of Wilde's conversation was his ability to play gracefully with philosophical ideas; we can imagine something of his intellectual range and agility if we turn to the Platonic dialogues he published in his collection of essays, *Intentions* (1891).

To these two popular conceptions of Wilde the talker – the prince of paradox and the first well-dressed philosopher in history – we must add a third. Wilde was the greatest storyteller of his age, and many of his friends believed that his particular genius best expressed itself in tales. Indeed, to one friend Wilde remarked that his ideas never came 'naked' into the world: 'I can *think*,' he said, 'in no other way save in stories. The sculptor does not translate his thought into marble; he thinks directly in marble.'

Wilde had an inexhaustible fund of stories. One friend described him as piling up tales around his armchair and then knocking them over with a loud laugh at the end of his performances. Another said that he seemed to have a miniature Scheherazade inside him who invented tale after tale in ways that he could neither control nor predict.

At dinner parties, when the meal ended and the coffee arrived, Wilde sometimes announced to the other guests: 'I have a new story.' More often, however, he was asked to tell a tale by a member of the company. 'And what, my dear boy,' he would say on these occasions, 'shall I tell you about?' On being given a topic such as 'Elizabethan England', or on being handed a jewel or a coin, he invented a tale on the subject or elaborated and embellished one he had told before. Then, in the murmur of appreciation that followed, he would be inspired by a comment to invent another tale. If his listeners were responsive, he would tell tale after tale for hours at a time, linking them with a witty commentary, as one listener wrote, like jewels held together on a golden chain. So famous did these performances become that hosts and hostesses wrote 'To meet Oscar Wilde and to listen to him tell a new story' on their invitation cards.

Some of Wilde's stories were based on humorous anecdotes about politicians or celebrities; others were poetical fables or adaptations of biblical tales. With one story he appealed to the intellect of his audience, with the next to its imagination, emotion or sense of the absurd. As he believed that conversation should touch on everything but concentrate on nothing, he never allowed a single theme or a single mood to dominate his discourse.

The effect of Wilde's stories on his audience was extraordinary. Many of his listeners wept openly while he narrated. More than one person described him as 'emitting rays' while talking. On one occasion, a guest actually screamed when she thought she saw a halo around his head. No one, it seems, was able to resist the enchanting spell he cast.

Most of those who heard Wilde narrate were convinced that his spoken stories were his greatest works. Up to the end of his life, his audiences urged him to write them down. It was probably at the request of his friends that he published six of his spoken stories in 1893–4 under the title *Poems in Prose*. His close friend and executor, Robert Ross, wrote later that the prose poems, which were 'the kind of story Wilde would tell at the dinner-table, being invented on the spur of the moment, or inspired by the chance observation of someone; or developed from some phrase in a book', were to have been continued. Yet, although letters from Wilde's final years contain tantalizing references to his having written down several 'new' prose poems, as far as we know, no other prose poems were published in his lifetime.

In the years immediately following his death, Wilde's friends lamented the fact that so many tales seemed to have died with the teller. It is clear that a few of them planned to write down and gather some stories into a single volume. In a letter to Robert Ross, for example, the artist William Rothenstein wrote: 'I was dining with York-Powell... and he suggested that something ought to be done with regard to preserving some of the most charming stories of Oscar… a small volume of table talk and the like.' Ross received similar suggestions from many of Wilde's friends but nothing was ever done; as a result, no such volume was published.

Fortunately, however, many of those who had heard Oscar Wilde did write down some of the spoken stories in their journals and notebooks. Some of these were later adapted as short stories, plays or poems; others were published in newspaper articles on Wilde or in books of reminiscence and autobiography. Some were written out in considerable detail soon after Wilde told them; others survive only as titles, as the faintest of outlines or in one or two fragmentary lines.

Many of these stories are familiar to Wilde-lovers, as writers such as Hesketh Pearson and Richard Ellmann have reproduced a number of them in their respective biographies. E. K. Mikhail's excellent *Oscar Wilde: Interviews and Recollections* (1979) also contains several lesser-known spoken stories that Wilde told during interviews with journalists or in conversation with friends. It was not, however, the specific intention of any of these authors to anthologize a substantial selection of Wilde's spoken stories. *Table Talk* is the first attempt in English to do so.

A comprehensive anthology of spoken stories was, however, published during the 1940s in French by the eccentric writer Guillot De Saix. Having read virtually everything written about Wilde, and after interviewing many of those who had known him during his final years in Paris, De Saix published over a hundred of Wilde's spoken stories. Although these vary greatly in quality and some are attributed to Wilde without any mention of sources, De Saix deserves praise for having preserved some of his finest tales. Some of these, along with several recorded by French novelist André Gide, have been translated and included in this book. Inevitably, given their 'oral' nature and uneven quality, De Saix's writings have sometimes been classed as 'apocrypha' by the literary establishment. However, as the reader will see, it is clear that Oscar Wilde told the stories selected for this book.

Most of the tales have been taken from autobiographies, English newspaper articles or memoirs of Wilde. Only fourteen have been translated from the French, a few for the first time. In general, the stories have been selected for their intrinsic quality and with the aim of making some of the lesser-known tales accessible to a wider audience.

Certain tales have been included for other reasons. Some cast an interesting light on Wilde's personality or his writing; there are those that reveal his fundamentally Celtic temperament, for example, while others allow us to understand something of his creative process.

The stories translated from French have also been chosen on the basis of their 'authenticity', in the sense that those selected were reported by people known to have met Wilde, or are mentioned by more than one source. We can be certain, for example, that Wilde told 'The Useless Resurrection'. It would be impossible and incongruous, however, to apply to these stories a traditional textual criterion of 'authenticity' because they belong to a completely separate genre: the oral narrative, or folk tale.

Folk tales have two main characteristics: they are usually adaptations of traditional stories, rather than 'original' works by a single author; and, as they are altered according to the company in which they are narrated, they generally lack fixed or 'definitive' form. Wilde's spoken stories display both these traits. Typically he retold a tale from the Bible, from history, mythology, literature, Irish folk tradition or even from his own works; he continually altered them according to the context in which they were told.

An essential part of Wilde's genius as a storyteller was, in fact, his almost telepathic sensitivity to his audience. To a poet, he told one of his tales as a complex philosophical fable; to a child, the same story would be transformed into an exciting tale of fantasy. Because of this, the following narratives should be thought of as the foundations upon which Wilde built completely new stories every time he told them. It is clear that, for him, they were quite simply *alive*.

It is hardly surprising, then, that most of the stories survive in a number of vastly different versions. The versions selected for this book are those that possess the greatest intrinsic quality or offer the reader the basic framework of each story. Having read them, the reader may then imagine the way in which Wilde would have embellished and reinvented a story according to the occasion.

In a sense, therefore, Wilde's listeners not only inspired him with their attention and applause, they also actively collaborated with him in the creation and the shaping of his tales. Thus it is very important to understand exactly when and where Wilde told his stories. To this end, each tale is prefaced by a description of the circumstances out of which it arose. Where this is unknown, the context in which another version of the same story was narrated, or a likely context for the story, has been provided. The story then follows.

The prefaces are not attempts to 'criticize' the stories. As a rule, they do not discuss the literary sources of the stories or their relationship to Wilde's written *oeuvre*. Nor do they offer suggestions for interpreting the tales. Wilde refused to 'explain' his tales. Indeed, he encouraged his listeners to participate actively in the creation of meaning, and used a number of strategies to keep that meaning ambiguous and indeterminate. In consequence, the prefaces aim to preserve rather than dispel the atmosphere of mystery and magic Wilde's performances created.

The prefaces do, however, sometimes relate the stories to more general aspects of Wilde's life and work; they also endeavour to bring to life the figure of Wilde in the act of telling the tales. In attempting to do this they follow a long tradition begun by many of Wilde's friends, who, after his death, found it necessary to evoke him by mimicking his mannerisms and his voice whenever they retold his tales in order to fully appreciate them. Even those who did not go to such lengths, such as the poet W. B. Yeats, had to imagine the way in which Wilde told his tales before they were able to savour them fully. And this, in a sense, is what we must do. As we read the stories, we should collaborate in their performance by trying to hear an echo of Wilde's 'golden voice' in our own.

The tales have been divided into three sections – 'Modern Stories & Anecdotes', 'Fables & Fairy Tales' and 'Biblical Tales' – arranged in a loose chronological order. Readers are encouraged, however, to read them in whatever sequence they prefer. It should be added that, as with a volume of poetry, *Table Talk* is not meant be read straight through at a single sitting.

*Oscar Wilde at the Royal Academy
in 1881. 'Society,' he predicted, 'will
return to its lost leader, the cultivated
and fascinating liar.'*

ANECDOTES

'It was an extraordinary improvisation…
He was brilliant, fantastic, irresponsible.
He charmed his listeners out of themselves,
and they followed his pipe laughing.'

THE PICTURE OF DORIAN GRAY

The Young Spendthrift

Oscar Wilde believed the possession of a musical voice to be the most indispensable attribute of a successful storyteller; having left Dublin for England, he assiduously set about acquiring one. Gradually he began to lose his rich Irish brogue – it was, he later said, one of the many things that he had forgotten at Oxford – and he replaced it with a clear and precise English society drawl.

His voice inspired more adjectives and metaphors than any of his other attributes. It was said to be warm, full, caressing, mossy, melodious, rich and languorous. One friend described it as a 'smooth-flowing utterance – sedate and self-possessed, oracular in tone – [that] carried on without halt, or hesitation'. Another remarked that the range and the music of Wilde's 'golden voice' had the power of transforming ordinary words into something 'exhilarating as wine'.

It is clear that the rhythm and sound of words were as important to Wilde as their meaning. He loved to accentuate the first syllable in words such as *'narcissus'*, *'amber'* and *'crimson'*; when he uttered 'vermilion' or 'marjoram', he enjoyed their sounds so much that he seemed to taste them. It is also evident that he used his voice to create ironic effects: he frequently narrated comic tales in a slow and solemn voice and told tales of fantasy as though relating everyday incidents.

There is, as Walter Pater said, 'something of the excellent talker' about Wilde's writing; as we read it, we seem to hear him speak. It is likely that he narrated these stories and anecdotes with the cadences and rhythms found in his short-story collection *Lord Arthur Savile's Crime and Other Stories* (1891).

H E WAS YOUNG AND HE WAS A POET. He lived a profligate and dissolute life in London, scattering around him the inheritance he had received from his father. When, after a while, he realized that he had reached his last few pounds and that he had accrued a number of considerable debts, his friends decided to rescue him.

Soon after, the most sincere and earnest of these friends came to inform him of their decision. 'Dear boy,' he announced, with the smile of a man who is thoroughly pleased with himself on account of his own good deeds, 'we have clubbed together and have resolved to pay all of your debts. What is more, if you promise to change your extravagant ways and to go and rebuild your ruined life in Australia, we will give you the sum of a hundred pounds.'

The young poet accepted the offer with profuse thanks. But, two months later, the same charitable friend came across the young spendthrift strolling through Piccadilly in a new set of fashionable clothes. The sight of the young man made his friend tremble with anger. Rushing over to the young spendthrift, he exclaimed, 'Good heavens, man! What the devil does this mean? You took the hundred pounds to go to Australia and now I find you idling around here dressed up like a damned dandy! I've never heard of such a thing in all my life! Tell me this instant why you have broken your word!'

When he heard this, the young spendthrift shrugged his shoulders nonchalantly and answered his friend with a question:

'And, tell *me*, dear boy: if *you* had a hundred pounds, would you go off to die in Australia?'

Aunt Jane's Ball

Wilde accompanied his tales with a repertoire of idiosyncratic mannerisms and gestures. Before beginning a story, he would throw his cigarette dramatically into the fire, or raise his arms into the air so that his hands shot out from his sleeves. While narrating, he continually moved his right hand in order to conjure up images and characters; with his left, he stroked his pale face or covered his nicotine-stained teeth when he laughed.

If a story lasted for more than a minute, Wilde would take a gold-tipped Egyptian cigarette out of one of his three silver cigarette cases with a flourish, light it and then wave it around in his right hand. As he moved his hand in the style of a conductor, the emerald scarab ring he wore on his finger sparkled through the monstrous flowers of smoke. During dramatic pauses, he raised his left hand until it became level with his right and blew smoke between them before continuing the tale.

It is easy to imagine Wilde in the company of others: serene and sphinx-like, a bent forefinger over his mouth while listening, animated yet deliberate when performing his tales. These performances also involved an element of mimicry. Wilde could evoke a character by a slight alteration in the tone of his voice or with the smallest movement of his eyes. While telling the following tale about 'his' Aunt Jane, he played the part of the affectionate nephew to perfection. 'Aunt Jane, Aunt Jane,' he began very slowly, as if to give himself time to visualize his latest imaginative creation. 'She was a very old lady,' he said, 'I hardly remember her myself…'

POOR AUNT JANE WAS VERY OLD and very proud, and she lived all alone in a splendid, desolate house in County Tipperary. None of her neighbours ever called on Aunt Jane and, had they done so, she would not have been pleased to see them. For she did not want anyone to see the overgrown drives of her estate, or the house with its faded chintzes and suites of shuttered rooms. And she could not bear the idea of anyone discovering that she herself was no longer a toast and a beauty, no longer a power in the countryside, but merely a lonely old woman who had outlived her day.

And so, from year to year she sat alone in her twilight, knowing nothing of the world outside. But one winter, even Aunt Jane became aware of a stir in the air, a wave of excitement that was sweeping over the neighbourhood. New people were coming into the new house on the hill, and they were going to give a great Ball, the like of which had never been seen. For the Ryans were enormously rich and – 'The Ryans?' said Aunt Jane. 'I don't know the Ryans. Where do they come from?' Then the terrible blow fell: the Ryans came from nowhere in particular and were reported on good authority to be 'in business'.

'But,' said Aunt Jane, 'what are the poor creatures thinking of? Who will ever go to their Ball?' 'Everybody will go,' she was assured. 'Everybody has accepted. It will be a wonderful affair.'

When Aunt Jane heard this, her wrath was terrible. *This* is what things had come to in the neighbourhood! And, of course, it was all her fault. After all, it had been for her to take the lead, but she had brooded in her tent when she should have been up doing battle.

Then Aunt Jane made a great resolution.

She would give a Ball – a Ball the like of which had never been imagined: she would re-enter Society and show how a *grande dame* of the old school could really entertain. If the County had so far forgotten itself, she herself would rescue it from those impertinent interlopers.

And so she instantly set to work. The old house was repainted and refurnished, and the grounds were replanted; the supper and the band were ordered from London and an army of waiters was engaged. She was determined that everything should be of the best – and that there should be no question of cost. She told herself that everything would eventually be paid for, even if she had to devote the rest of her life to paying for it.

At last, the great night arrived. The estate was lit for miles around with coloured lamps, the hall and the staircase were gorgeous with flowers, and the dancing floor was as smooth and as shiny as a mirror. Then, from their places, the musicians bowed deeply as Aunt Jane, in a splendid gown embroidered with diamonds, descended in state and stood at the ballroom door.

There she waited. And, as time went on, the footmen in the hall and the waiters in the supper-room began to look at each other, and the band tuned up two or three times to show its zeal, but no guests arrived.

And still Aunt Jane, in her beautiful gown, waited at the ballroom door. The clock struck eleven – twelve – half-past twelve and still no guests arrived.

At last, Aunt Jane swept a deep curtsy to the band. 'Pray go and have your supper,' she said. 'No one is coming.' Then she went upstairs and died. That is to say, she never again spoke a word to anyone and was dead within three days.

And not for some time after her death was it discovered that Aunt Jane had quite forgotten to send out any invitations.

The Young Inventor

As soon as he began to speak, even those who found Oscar Wilde's appearance unattractive could not remain impervious to his charm. This effect was due partly to his musical voice, and partly to his laughter and his soulful eyes. His laughter, which always accompanied and sometimes even preceded his jokes, was the loud and infectious laughter of a contented ogre – or of an adult who had somehow managed to remain a child. His eyes, which were variously described as playful, childlike or dreamy, seemed to penetrate his listeners' souls.

With these attributes Wilde was able to overpower and seduce everyone he met: publishers, politicians, children, prisoners, beggars, poets, urchins, barristers, animals, anarchists and adversaries. Even George Bernard Shaw, a man so utterly dissimilar to Wilde, was enthralled when they met by chance at an exhibition in Chelsea.

'It was,' recalled Shaw, 'my sole experience of Oscar's wonderful gift as a raconteur… and I understood why [William] Morris, when he was dying slowly, enjoyed a visit from Wilde more than from anybody else.' During their conversation, Wilde told many elaborate tales, but the only one that Shaw was able to recall in any detail was 'The Young Inventor'.

A YOUNG MAN INVENTED A THEATRE STALL that economized space by ingenious contrivances. A friend of his invited twenty millionaires to meet him at a dinner so that he might interest them in the invention. At the dinner, the young man succeeded in convincing the millionaires by his demonstration of the savings in a theatre holding, in ordinary seats, six hundred; this made them eager and ready to make his fortune.

Unfortunately, however, the young man then went on to calculate the annual savings in all the theatres of the world, then in all the churches of the world, then in all the legislatures, estimating finally the incidental moral and religious effects of the invention until, at the end of an hour, he had estimated a profit of several thousands and millions.

The consequence of all of this was, of course, that the millionaires folded their tents and silently stole away, leaving the ruined inventor a marked man for life.

The Actress

Wilde narrated the following story on several occasions and characteristically told it in a different way each time. One friend who heard 'The Actress' said that it later inspired Wilde's account of Sybil Vane in *The Picture of Dorian Gray* (1891). The protagonist of the following version, however, bears only a superficial similarity to that character. The story was written down in the early 1890s by two women who probably heard it at one of the Wildes' Tite Street (in Chelsea, London) dinners.

At these dinners, Wilde sometimes obliged his wife by entertaining her friends with anecdotes and tales. Ever the spendthrift of his own genius, he exerted himself in front of such audiences as though they were great poets or groups of his closest friends. This is no doubt partly due to the fact that Wilde felt a compulsion to narrate, but it is also because he knew that his own invention was inexhaustible. It is one of the reasons why Wilde was the least proprietorial of authors: he gave away plots and ideas to those around him just as he gave away his money. On one occasion at Tite Street, he charmed his listeners so much that, like the men in Greek mythology who were ravished by the muses, they were unable to taste their food.

The actress and 'princess of beautiful postures and gestures'
Sarah Bernhardt, whose voice Wilde is said to have imitated.

T HERE WAS ONCE A VERY GREAT ACTRESS who had so perfected her art that the whole of the theatrical world worshipped at her feet. Like all artists of genius, her art became for her the one reality of life, and she had absolutely no curiosity for the world outside the theatre.

One day, however, she met a man with whom she fell passionately in love. Then all her art, and even the adoration of the audience, became as nothing to her. But, even though she assured her lover that her heart belonged entirely to him, he grew terribly jealous of a public for which the woman no longer cared. So, one day, when he could bear his jealousy no longer, he implored her to leave the stage.

Now, as her love had already made the actress half-sick of the theatre and its unreal shadows, she was able to sacrifice her art without too much difficulty. 'Love is better than art,' she said to herself, 'better than fame, better than life itself.' And so she decided to leave the stage and all her marvellous triumphs in order to dedicate herself solely to the man she loved.

Time passed, and although in the beginning they were blissfully happy, after a while the man's love began to wither and die. It was, of course, impossible for him to conceal this from the woman who had given up everything for him. The knowledge that the man no longer loved her fell upon the actress like a chill mist at evening, and wrapped her from head to foot in a grey shroud of despair.

But, being a brave woman, she forced herself to look directly at the situation, even though the clarity with which she saw it cut into her heart. Not only did she see clearly that the man no longer loved her, but it was also patently obvious that she had made a dreadful mistake in sacrificing her art for their love. And with equal clarity she also saw that, instead of being an inspiration and an aid in her hour of need, her art was in fact a hindrance to her. For now that she was called upon to grapple with reality, she missed the stage manager's directions and the author's words. Until now, she had never done anything without them, and she discovered to her horror that she was utterly incapable of acting in the real world.

Then one day, as she was pacing up and down in her drawing room, the manager of the theatre in which she had acted came to visit her. The leading lady of the play he was putting on at that time had suddenly fallen ill and, in his desperation, he had come to ask the actress if she would play the part as a favour to him. As she had not acted for some time and now that she realized her art had failed her, the actress refused. 'What have I,' she said to him, 'to do with the puppets of the play, and the painted scenes and the empty pageants?' However, as it meant a great deal of money to him, the manager persisted. Would she not at least *read* the play?

If only to be rid of him, the actress agreed. After having read only a few pages, she was astonished to discover that the tragedy

Caricature of Wilde by 'Oliver Paque' (W. H. Pike)
from The Daily Graphic *in 1890.*

of the play was identical to the tragedy of her life. The characters and the plot were exactly the same, and in the denouement of the play a solution to her problem was also given.

Thus Fate had come to the actress's aid in the form of a play, and she decided to take the part in order to master every detail of the situation. So she studied the part and soon played it in front of a large audience. Her performance was, without doubt, the greatest of her entire career, and at the end of the play, she received four standing ovations and nine bouquets.

When it was all over, she left the theatre with the shouts of the audience still ringing in her ears. As she had poured out her soul before the audience, a profound weariness threatened to overcome her as she arrived at her front door laden with flowers.

On entering the house, she suddenly noticed that two places had been laid at the supper table. Then she remembered that tonight was the night that would decide her fate.

At that very moment, the man she had loved so passionately and for whom she had sacrificed her art sauntered into the room. With a smile he asked her if he was in time for supper.

Looking at the clock, she replied, 'You are in time for supper. But –' she added, staring directly into his eyes, 'you are also just too late.'

Presence of Mind

'Presence of Mind' is an exemplary oral narrative. It is a tale common to many folk traditions, which Wilde adapted in his own idiosyncratic way; he also altered it every time it was told. In one version of the story, his protagonist is a flute-player; in the more elaborate version given here, the flute-player has been transformed into an actor. The reason for this is very simple: Wilde told the tale at a lunch party given by his theatrical friends. The outline of the two versions is roughly the same but, within that basic structure, he was able to create an entirely new tale.

As usual, Wilde arrived late at the lunch party. He said that he had been busy writing the first volume of *The People's Cheap Guinea Series of Great Thoughts*. 'The subject,' he said, 'has occupied every minute I could spare from eating, drinking and sleeping.' Having gained the attention of the entire table with his ingenious but obviously insincere apology, he went on: '[It will be] a small volume of moral essays. The first essay, on which I am now engaged, deals with the value of presence of mind, and is in the form of an anecdote… [It is based on] an incident from real life which was related to me by a well-known actor, still happily amongst us, who owes his very existence to a daring exhibition of coolness in the face of terrible danger.' He then began the following tale.

M Y YOUNG FRIEND THE ACTOR was playing the chief part in an extremely popular drama. For months there had not been an empty seat in the house, and at every performance the queues for the pit and gallery stretched for miles: indeed, they stretched as far as Hammersmith. (I ought to add, however, that the play was being performed *at* Hammersmith.)

One evening during the performance, at the excruciatingly tense moment when the poor flower-girl rejects with scorn the odious proposals of the wicked marquis, a huge cloud of smoke poured from the wings and the scenery was caught by great tongues of fire.

Although the safety curtain was immediately lowered, the audience was terrified and dashed towards the exits. A hideous panic broke out – the men started shouting and pushing, and the women began to scream and clutch at one another. There was a serious danger that many would be trampled to death, and in fact, some skirts were soiled, and several dress shirts were crumpled.

At the height of the din, my young actor friend – who, in the play, loves and is loved by the flower-girl – came up through the orchestra door, took in the situation at a glance, and scrambled onto the stage. There, in front of the iron curtain, standing erect with flashing eyes and with his arm upraised, he commanded silence in a voice which rang like a trumpet through the theatre. The audience knew that voice well, and felt reassured: the panic immediately subsided.

Oscar Wilde at Magdalen College, Oxford, in 1876. According to a fellow undergraduate, 'the romantic imagination was strong in him'.

Then he told them that there was no longer any danger from the fire, which was now completely under control. He went on to say that there was, however, a very real danger from their own fear. He told them that as their lives depended upon keeping their heads they must return to their seats at once.

Feeling thoroughly ashamed of themselves, they did as they were told. And when the exits were clear and all the seats occupied once more, the actor leapt lightly over the footlights into the stalls and vanished through the first convenient doorway. Then the auditorium filled with smoke; the flames raced in from every side; and not another soul left the place alive.

Thus we may see how useful a thing presence of mind really is.

Lord Arthur Savile and the Palmist

Nearly all Oscar Wilde's written works began as spoken stories; he told endless versions of his fairy tales and *The Picture of Dorian Gray*, for example, over many years before he wrote them down. He even narrated his plays as stories, and most of his dialogues and essays grew out of dinners with friends; one acquaintance suggested that he even talked while writing. Wilde, it seems, conceived all his works in conversation; he was a poet who only became inspired in public.

Those who heard him narrate were invariably disappointed when they read his works. To his listeners, the stories lost some of their vitality in the translation from the spoken to the written word. This was certainly the conclusion of those who heard and then read the story that is familiar to us as 'Lord Arthur Savile's Crime', a tale Wilde told a number of times before its first publication in 1887.

On one of these occasions, he was walking (without much enthusiasm) in the country with his friend the painter Graham Robertson. Spying a seat, Wilde implored Robertson to let him sit down. 'Look here,' he said, 'if you'll let me sit down I'll tell you a story. Did I ever tell you about George Ellison and the palmist?' He then proceeded to tell him a version of 'Lord Arthur Savile's Crime'. On another occasion, Wilde narrated a different version of the story in the studio of the artist Bernard Partridge. After the hour-long recital, Partridge urged him to write it down. 'I don't think I will,' Wilde replied wearily. 'It's such a bore writing things out.'

The following version of the story, one of many Wilde told at a lunch party, was apparently narrated in less than five minutes.

I T WAS AT LADY THIRLMERE'S GREAT RECEPTION that Lord Arthur Savile met Mr. Ransom, the palmist. He had always wanted to know what the future held in store for him, and he watched the palmist inspect his hand with an interest he could hardly conceal. Mr. Ransom frowned and looked uncomfortable; then he trembled, his complexion turned white, and his voice shook. 'You are fated to kill someone,' he whispered to Lord Arthur, 'and you cannot escape your fate.'

By the time Lord Arthur recovered from the shock, Mr. Ransom had disappeared. It was indeed an unpleasant predicament to find oneself in, but Lord Arthur reflected that it would be still more unpleasant for the person he had to kill and, naturally, this thought consoled him. His real difficulty as a gentle and good-natured young man was to kill his victim as quickly and as painlessly as he possibly could. Surely nothing could be simpler, he thought to himself. But he was to discover that things were not quite so simple as that.

For the clergyman whom he tried to push under the wheels of an omnibus stepped back suddenly, trod on Lord Arthur's feet, and went away without apologizing. The next attempt was an even more dismal failure. He sent some poison by post to an uncle who had been ill for a long time, and from whose will he expected to benefit. But what is one man's poison is another man's cure, and a fortnight later his uncle gave a dinner-party to celebrate his return to health.

Then, while driving his dogcart in Hyde Park one morning, Lord Arthur saw a man leave the path and start to walk slowly across the road. As he appeared to be an invalid, Lord Arthur

Wilde at the theatre, by Maurice Greiffenhagen. Even as a member of the audience, he still managed to attract one of his own.

was not only hopeful of success but also happy in the knowledge that he would be serving the cause of humanity by killing the man. So he whipped up his horse and drove straight at the man, but the man, thinking that it was a runaway carriage, jumped lightly to one side, seized the bridle, and brought the horse to a standstill. Lord Arthur had to tip him a sovereign.

Again and again his attempts to commit murder were frustrated. The explosive he sent to an aunt did not explode; the lady he tripped into a canal was saved by a passer-by, and both of them had to be recompensed; the child he overturned in a pram was highly entertained – and asked Lord Arthur to do it again. It really seemed that Fate was against him.

But, one night, while he was walking along the Thames Embankment in despair and wondering whether suicide would count as murder, he saw a man leaning over the parapet. No one was in sight and the river was in flood. It was indeed a heaven-sent opportunity. And so, leaning down quickly, he seized the unknown man's legs. There was a splash in the dark, swirling waters, and then peace descended upon Lord Arthur. His duty done, he slept well, and did not rise again until the following afternoon.

One of the first things to catch his eye as he opened the newspaper he always read at breakfast was a paragraph headed: 'Well-known Palmist drowned – Suicide of Mr. Ransom'. And, when the day of Mr. Ransom's funeral arrived, Lord Arthur sent him a wreath, on which the words 'In Gratitude' were inscribed.

The Glass Eye

The effect of Wilde's stories was sometimes likened to that of enchanting music; more often, however, it was compared to that of sunlight. His very presence seemed to radiate warmth and a sense of well-being to those around him; his enormous capacity for joy and his sense of wonder were irresistible and infectious.

One of Wilde's friends said that he had never before encountered someone so completely in harmony with himself, or someone who had such a gift for living entirely in the present moment. Another acquaintance remarked that the genuine and spontaneous delight Wilde took in his own inventions was an essential part of his charm. One of his greatest pleasures was to look on as, little by little, every face in a room turned towards him.

Once he had gained the complete attention of his audience, Wilde would take up a subject and play with it in the manner of his own creation from *The Picture of Dorian Gray*, Lord Henry Wotton: 'He grew wilful; tossed it into the air and transformed it; let it escape and recaptured it; made it iridescent with fancy and winged it with paradox.' Sometimes he asked his listeners for a subject; at others he began a fantastic improvisation after hearing a quotation, a trivial remark or an item of news.

Wilde probably invented the following story after hearing from a member of his audience the details of a real accident – 'a bomb explosion in a restaurant' – in which an enemy of his had lost an eye.

ONCE A VERY VAIN AND VERY RICH young gentleman had the misfortune to lose one of his eyes in a dreadful hunting accident. Soon after the accident, he decided that he would have made for himself the most beautiful glass eye in the world. It would, he hoped, be in every respect a glass eye worthy of his wealth, personal beauty and name.

And so, out of the rarest pure crystal and the finest enamel, the miniature masterpiece was wrought. The shadowy pupil seemed to have been made out of velvet, and in the deep-green waters of the iris sparkled tiny flakes of gold. When the rich young gentleman gazed at his glass eye in front of one of his many mirrors, he was so satisfied with it that he half fell in love with himself once more.

After a while, in order to put the glass eye to the test, he invited his closest friend round for afternoon tea. Of course, during their conversation, the rich young man expected to be showered with compliments about the beauty of his marvellous new eye, but, when he realized that these were not forthcoming, he asked his friend directly what he thought of it.

Alas, when the friend examined it closely, he was less than impressed. 'Well, all things considered,' he said half-heartedly, 'it suits you rather well, old boy. It is indeed a charming thing, and no doubt the very best of its kind.'

'Good God, man!' exclaimed the rich young gentleman. 'Is that really all you can say? Evidently you know nothing at all about these things! Aren't you astonished at how life like it is? For my own part, I assure you,

I think it so marvellous that I find myself scarcely able to distinguish between it and my real eye. *Do* look at my eyes again, like a good boy, and tell me in all honesty if you are able to identify the glass eye.'

But, much to the astonishment of the rich young gentleman, his friend was able to identify the artificial eye without a moment's hesitation. On being asked how he had recognized it so quickly, he said, somewhat disingenuously, 'Because, of your two eyes, it is by far the most beautiful.'

'Ah!' said the rich young gentleman. 'That may be so, but that is not the real reason. The fact is you were only able to recognize it because you knew beforehand which eye I had lost in that damned accident. And in order to convince you that I am right, let us go out together into the streets and conduct a little experiment. What do you say to this? We'll stop the first person who happens to pass by and ask him to see if he can distinguish between the glass eye and the real one.'

Having agreed to a 'gentleman's wager' over the matter, the two men went out together into the street. There, leaning up against a nearby wall, they saw a miserable beggar; he was one of those poor men whose spirits have sunk so low that they are unable to summon up enough courage even to ask for money when the rich pass by. Indeed, he looked so forlorn and wretched that the friend of the rich young gentleman felt sorry for him.

The rich young gentleman sauntered over to where the beggar was standing and asked him, with an air of extreme condescension, whether or not he wanted to earn a crown.

'A crown, sir!' replied the beggar. 'That would go down very well with me, because, the truth is, sir, I haven't eaten for days.'

Having explained to the beggar exactly what he had to do, the rich young gentleman stood directly in front of him. And, nonchalantly tossing a crown into the beggar's hand, he said, 'Now, my fine fellow: take as long as you like over it, and when you have quite made up your mind, tell me which of my eyes is the glass eye.'

The beggar did not need to take very long to come to his decision; after one or two seconds, he pointed out the artificial eye. The rich young man stepped back from him in amazement and asked him how he had been able to identify it so easily.

'It is – if I may be so bold, sir – a very simple matter,' the beggar answered. 'Your glass eye is the only one in which I can see any pity.'

The True History of Anne of Cleves

Wilde believed that it part of his social mission to return to English society its lost leader: the incorrigible, fascinating liar. The imaginative stories he narrated after lunches and dinners to aristocrats, MPs and journalists were part of this endeavour. Because he thought of these occasions as ceremonies rather than feasts, he usually waited until the coffee arrived before beginning his performance. At this time, the host or hostess announced to the other guests, 'Now, Oscar Wilde is going to tell us one of his latest stories.'

Wilde based some of these tales on events from English history. It was typical of him to take an incident from 'official' history and give it his own imaginative version. Naturally, he thought objective 'facts' and 'authentic' historical 'truths' were illusions; he also believed that, in the works of official history, they usurped the domain of fancy and invaded the kingdom of romance.

One of Wilde's greatest gifts as a raconteur was his ability to make his stories seem part of the general conversation. Frequently, they were suggested by the comments of others; sometimes, he even used the rudest interruption as the starting point for new flights of fancy. On this particular occasion, he was sitting with an impassive and mask-like face, listening to a discourse on the notorious ugliness of Anne of Cleves. Suddenly, his large, dreamy eyes lit up under their heavy lids. 'You believe she was really ugly?' he exclaimed. 'No, my dear boy, she was as exquisite as we see her in the Louvre.' And with typical animation, he recounted the following tale.

A LONG WITH THE ESCORT which brought Anne of Cleves to England, there travelled a beautiful young nobleman. After some time, Anne became passionately enamoured of the man and, on the ship, they became lovers.

But what could be done? Discovery would, of course, mean death. So Anne stained her face, and put uncouth clothes upon her body, until she resembled the ugly monster Henry thought her when they met.

Now, do you know what happened? Years passed, and one day, when the king went hawking, he heard a woman singing in an orchard close by.

And, rising in his stirrups to see who had so entranced him with her lovely voice, he beheld Anne of Cleves, young and beautiful, singing in the arms of her lover.

The Magic Ball

Like Doctor Chasuble's sermon on the meaning of the manna in the desert (alluded to in *The Importance of Being Earnest*, 1895) Wilde's stories could be adapted to almost any occasion. As a result, stories such as 'The Magic Ball' survive in a multiplicity of versions.

The most elaborate version of the story was told to the editor Frank Harris, who later adapted it and published it as a short story. This version, which concerns a scientist who discovers that the laws of thought are the same as the laws of physics, is a complicated philosophical fable that Wilde probably adapted to Harris's intellectual tastes. Another, completely different and far more comic version involves a magician who travels to England to demonstrate the discovery of spontaneous movement to the king.

The following version is by far the simplest. Wilde told it to his friend Louis Latourette in 1898. Although it dates from the last years of his life, it is evident that he told a version of it, which he sometimes called 'The Sphere', to friends such as More Adey, Robert Ross and the novelist Robert Hichens in the early Nineties.

ONCE THERE WAS A FAMOUS SCIENTIST who discovered the secret of spontaneous movement. One day, in order to make public his extraordinary discovery, he decided to organize a demonstration during which he would place a large ball on a perfectly horizontal level, and make it move entirely of its own accord. Having made all the necessary preparations, he sent out invitations to the academicians of his country, the parliament and the king.

But, on the morning before the demonstration, the scientist grew nervous and began to wonder if he had made a mistake in one of his calculations. He realized, of course, that failure in front of such an audience would destroy the great reputation he had spent years in building for himself.

As he sat alone pondering these weighty matters, a young boy passed by in front of him. On seeing the young boy, a wonderful idea came into the scientist's head, and he called the boy over to him.

'You like marbles and sweets and spinning tops, don't you?' he said to the young boy. 'Now, I will give you all of these things if you promise to do one small favour for me. What you must do is this: in about two and a half hours' time, I want you to go to the big park in the centre of the town. When you get there you will see a very large ball. Now, this ball is hollow inside, and what you must do is climb into it through a tiny trapdoor at the top. Until you hear me come into the park with lots of other men, you must stay perfectly still inside of the ball and as quiet as a mouse. And when we have all arrived in the park, I want you to listen very carefully because, after a little while, in a very low voice, I will say, "Roll, ball." And when you hear me say this, what you must do is move around inside the ball so that it will roll. And that, young sir, is all there is to it. If you do everything I have told you to do, then you can have as many marbles and sweets as you like. Now, have you understood what I have said?'

'Yes, sir,' said the boy with a smile. 'I know just what to do.'

So, later that day, the academicians of the country, along with the parliament and the king, gathered together in the park to see the scientist's demonstration.

And when the scientist said 'Roll, ball!' the ball rolled, and everyone stared in amazement. 'It's a miracle!' they all cried out, and then they clapped their hands and cheered.

But, while the loud applause was ringing in his ears, the scientist suddenly broke down and started to cry. And through his tears, he confessed to the audience that he had tricked them.

'Forgive me, people; forgive me, your majesty,' he said, 'but I have been cheating you all along. My scientific conscience is stronger than my vanity and I must confess to you that I don't know whether or not I have discovered spontaneous movement. Yes, the ball did roll in front of your eyes, but that was because there was a child inside it.'

A chorus of insults and boos came from the audience, and the enraged king stood up and shouted at the scientist: 'Impostor! You have made a mockery of the great scientific reputation of this country! For this you will spend the rest of your life locked up in jail. Guards: take the charlatan away!'

Accompanied by the curses and the sarcastic jeers of the people, the crestfallen scientist made his way to jail. Now, along the way he passed by a gang of children playing hopscotch, and among them he saw the young boy who had promised to go inside the ball. Turning round to find out what all the commotion was about the young boy saw the scientist surrounded by the guards and ran over to him.

'Sir, it's me! You remember me?' he said, 'I'm the one you talked to this morning about the sweets and the ball and all those other things. I'm really sorry, sir, for what I did, but here I was playing hopscotch with my friends and I forgot all about going to the park and getting inside the ball and everything. So please don't be cross with me, sir – if you only knew what great fun this game of hopscotch has been – well, if you knew that, then I reckon you'd still give me the marbles and spinning tops and the sweets anyway…'

On hearing this, the scientist bent down and patted the cheek of the boy and gave him a golden coin with which to buy the marbles and the sweets. Then, without a word, and with a triumphant smile on his face, he walked off slowly towards the jail.

Wilde, drawn by Thomas Maitland Cleland (1884). He often appeared half-asleep when telling stories.

FABLES

*'In art there is no such thing as a
universal truth. A truth in art is that
whose contradictory is also true.'*

The House of Judgement

Oscar Wilde once remarked that it was the duty of every father to invent fairy tales for his children. Whenever he tired of playing in the nursery at Tite Street, he would entertain his two young boys with stories. He narrated tales of adventure in the manner of Robert Louis Stevenson, the Irish folk tales his parents had told him, and all of his famous fairy tales. One night, after Wilde had been telling 'The Selfish Giant', his eldest son Cyril noticed that he had tears in his eyes. When he asked him why he was crying, Wilde said that really beautiful things always made him cry.

Wilde's youngest son, Vyvyan, later remembered that his father told him and his brother hundreds of tales. There was one story about some fairies who lived in the great bottles of coloured water chemists used to put in their windows and who, at night, danced around and made pills in the empty shop.

Vyvyan was unable to recollect any of the tales in their entirety, but he did say that Wilde also narrated to them many of the complicated fables he would later write down as 'prose poems'. Although he and his brother rarely understood these stories, Vyvyan remarked that they always kept them spellbound. It is very likely then that Wilde told his boys 'The House of Judgement', a story based upon a traditional Irish folk tale called 'The Priest's Soul', which Wilde's mother had reproduced in one of her books on Irish folklore.

AND THERE WAS A GREAT SILENCE in the House of Judgement. And the soul of the man stood naked before God.

And God opened the book of the man's life and said, 'Surely thou hast been very evil. Since thou hast done all these things, even into hell will I send thee.'

And the man cried out, 'Thou canst not send me into hell.'

And God said, 'Wherefore can I not send thee into hell?' And the man answered, 'Because in hell I have always lived.'

And there was a great silence in the House of Judgement.

And God said to the man, 'Seeing that I may not send thee into hell, even into heaven will I send thee.'

And the man said, 'Thou canst not send me into heaven.'

And God said, 'Wherefore can I not send thee into heaven?' And the man said, 'Because I have never been able to imagine it.'

And there was a great silence in the House of Judgement.

The Illusion of Free Will

Oscar Wilde had a great gift for telling stories to children, and many of those who heard him during their childhood recalled the effect, if not the details, for the rest of their lives. One woman remembered 'his indolent figure, lounging in an easy chair, his face alive with delight in what he was saying... He had a way of looking at one to see how much nonsense one would believe; if you showed signs of scepticism he would say in mock sadness, "You don't believe me, Miss Nelly? I *assure* you... well, it's as good as true."'

Wilde never condescended to children by telling them 'childish' tales: he adapted for them exactly the same fables and biblical parables he told to poets and politicians. Similarly, he frequently told fairy tales to adults that contained talking animals and mythical creatures – tales that were suffused with a humour that was childlike in its lightness and absurdity. Wilde once said that his tales were invented for all children from the ages of eighteen to eighty; and indeed, he was able to reawaken a childlike sense of wonder in adult listeners. After having discussed politics or philosophy over dinner, they would sit like enraptured children at Wilde's feet when the coffee was served.

The following story is an example of a fable that was undoubtedly told to both children and adults. According to the friend who heard it, Wilde invented it spontaneously while they were discussing the idea of free will.

Wilde's sons, Cyril (left) and Vyvyan. Not
surprisingly, the master storyteller exercised the
power of the Pied Piper over children.

ONCE UPON A TIME THERE WAS A MAGNET who lived near some steel filings. One day some of the tiniest of the filings felt a sudden urge to pay the magnet a visit. However, as the grown-up filings were very strict indeed, the tiny filings were not allowed to go anywhere by themselves. So they tried to convince the grown-up filings to go along to visit the magnet with them.

On hearing their plan, the grown-ups became so excited about it that they told all their friends and relatives who lived in the neighbourhood next to them. And when they had all come together, they began to discuss exactly when they ought to go. The tiniest filings, who were by now feeling very impatient, cried out, 'Why not go today?' But some of the older and the more indolent among them were of the opinion that it would be better to wait until the following morning.

Now, while they were all chatting away together, they had, without realizing it, been moving nearer and nearer to the magnet all the time. And, as they went on arguing about when to set off on their long and arduous journey, they moved closer and closer still. The magnet, who had been watching them for a while now, lay there quite motionless, apparently taking no heed of them.

And the more the filings discussed the matter, the more their desire to visit the magnet grew, until the tiniest filings, who by this time had had quite enough of waiting, declared that they would go that very instant. To their astonishment the very oldest among the filings agreed with them and were even heard to say that it was their duty to visit the magnet at once. And, while they talked, still they moved nearer and nearer to the magnet, without knowing anything about it.

Then finally the tiniest filings prevailed, and, in a loud voice all the filings cried out: 'There is no use waiting! We will go today! We will go now! We will go at once!' So, in one body, the filings flew through the air, and in less than a second they were clinging fast to every side of the magnet.

Then a smile lit up the magnet's face and he began to laugh quietly to himself. For even now that the filings were stuck so fast to his body that they could not move at all, it was obvious to him from their conversation that they still believed that they were paying him a visit entirely of their own free will.

The Rose of the Infanta

Oscar Wilde once remarked that a man who could dominate a London dinner table could also dominate the world; on another occasion he added that no man could ever succeed in doing so unless he had society women to back him. Perhaps this is why Wilde himself spent a great deal of time charming aristocratic ladies with his fairy tales.

All of the stories in Wilde's second volume of fairy tales, *A House of Pomegranates* (1891), were dedicated to the society hostesses to whom he had told them, as a 'slight' return for their hospitality. In a typical letter which accompanied a book of short stories, Wilde wrote to one of these women, 'I am sending you a little book that contains a story, two stories in fact, that I told you at Taplow…'

None of these women wrote down any of Wilde's tales; fortunately, however, he also told fairy stories to other friends. On a visit to Cambridge in 1885, for example, Wilde told 'The Happy Prince' at a dinner with some undergraduates. His audience seemed so entranced by the story that, on returning to his room, he decided to write it down.

He told a version of 'The Birthday of the Infanta' to a female friend. The woman was, alas, able to set down only the following outline of the tale in her diary. 'By the by,' she wrote, '[Wilde] told me a whole story of the *Infanta* of Velásquez in the Louvre, with a pink rose in her hand. He was bent on learning the history of that rose, and found it in a portrait near at hand, of a dwarf.'

A ND WHEN THE DWARF DANCED in front of the court, the princess, who had laughed heartily at the dwarf's grotesqueness, took a pink rose from her hair and flung it to him in jest. Then she ordered the dwarf to dance again for her later on the same day.

Now the dwarf, who had passed all of his life in the forest and who was completely unaware of his own ugliness, took the matter very seriously indeed. And, walking away from the palace with the pink rose in his hand, he was full of rapture at the thought that the beautiful princess was in love with him.

When the dwarf returned to the palace later that afternoon, he happened to enter a room full of mirrors. Although for a few moments he failed to recognize his own reflection in one of the mirrors, at length he realized, for the very first time in his life, the hideousness of his deformed body and the ugliness of his face. With a wild cry of despair, he fell down to the ground.

After a while, the princess and her friends came into the room full of mirrors. Seeing the dwarf, and remembering the pleasure they had taken in his antics, they entreated him to dance. But the dwarf remained silent and motionless on the floor. And, when they finally realized what had happened, the princess's friends said to her, 'He is dead – dead of a broken heart.' Turning away from the dwarf, the princess announced haughtily: 'Henceforth, let those who love me have no hearts.'

The Face of the Soul

Frank Harris frequently gave lunch parties at his house in Park Lane or at Claridge's in London. He would invite artists, royalty, aristocrats and writers, one of whom recorded his impressions of a lunch that Wilde also attended. At first, all the guests talked to their neighbours, but gradually, as the meal went on, Wilde's infectious laugh and musical voice began to sound more clearly as, one by one, they fell silent to listen to him.

First one hour passed, and then another as Wilde narrated tale after tale. He told humorous anecdotes, terrifying Gothic stories inspired by Edgar Allan Poe such as the following, the outlines of plays he intended to write down and the biblical stories that Harris would later publish as *Poems in Prose* in *The Fortnightly Review* (1894). When, with a wave of the hand, Wilde finally ceased to speak, his listeners decided that any further conversation would be an anticlimax and gathered round to congratulate him.

Wilde's performances at these lunches (which sometimes lasted from two o'clock in the afternoon until nine o'clock in the evening) were not quite as effortless as they appeared. 'I had to strain every nerve,' he would confess to friends afterwards; and to Harris he wrote, 'In your luncheon-parties... the remains of the guests were taken away with the debris of the feast. I have often lunched with you in Park Lane and found myself the only survivor.'

I N HIS PROFLIGATE YOUTH, a man saw a being that hid its face from him, and the man thought, 'I will compel it to show its face.' But the being fled as he pursued it, and he lost it, and his sinful life went on.

After many years had passed, the man's pleasure drew him into a long room, where the tables were lavishly spread with food and wine. In a mirror that stood in the corner of the room he saw the being that he had pursued in his youth.

'This time you shall not escape me!' he cried, but the being did not try to escape, and hid its face no more. 'Look!' it cried. 'And then you will understand that we cannot see each other again, for this is the face of your soul, and it is horrible!'

The young Wilde, circa 1882. According to one listener,
'One might not press Wilde too closely for the meaning of his stories.'

The Poet

Wilde's 'golden voice' was used to great effect when he told fables such as 'The Poet'. At dramatic moments he would lower it to a whisper as though imparting a great secret to his audience; while enumerating the splendours in his descriptive passages, he used a stately monotone. Some listeners thought that Wilde seemed dazed (or even half-asleep) as he narrated. Others described him as listening attentively to the stories and marvelling at his own invention as he went along.

The rhythms of Wilde's prose poems, his long prison letter *De Profundis* (1905) and plays such as *Salome* (1893) capture something of the majestic and musical tone with which he told his fables, fairy tales and biblical stories. The cadences and rhythms he used were largely inspired by the King James Bible, a book from which he loved to quote long, elaborate phrases.

Wilde told at least six different versions of 'The Poet', repeating it frequently from its conception in around 1889 right up to his death in 1900. (From his letters and a recently discovered manuscript outline, it is also clear that he intended to write it down.) In most of these, the protagonist is a poet, but in others he is a storyteller or a fisher boy. Sometimes Wilde included a scene in which the poet's disappointed audience stones him to death; sometimes he ended it with the words, 'To a poet, fancy is reality – and reality is nothing.' Usually, however, he concluded with the poet's phrase, 'Today I have seen nothing,' and then burst out laughing as his listeners pondered the meaning of the tale.

The French novelist André Gide gives an example of the way in which Wilde introduced 'The Poet'. Having asked what Gide had been doing the previous day, Wilde received an answer that he found rather banal. 'Then why tell it?' he asked. 'You must see yourself that all that is very uninteresting. There are just two worlds: the one that exists without one ever speaking of it, called the real world... the other is the world of art: one must talk of that, for without such talk, it would not exist.'

'The Poet' was inspired by an Irish folk tale called 'The Storyteller at Fault'. When Wilde narrated this version to the artist Charles Ricketts, he conjured up the image of the retreating centaur with an imperceptible turn of his head.

NOW, A CERTAIN YOUNG MAN was greatly loved by the people of his village, for, when they gathered round him at dusk and questioned him, he would relate to them the many strange things he had seen during the day.

He would say, 'I beheld three mermaids by the sea, who combed their green hair with a golden comb.' And when they besought him to tell them more, he answered, 'By a hollow rock I spied a centaur, and when his eyes met mine, he turned slowly to depart, gazing at me sadly over his shoulder.' And when they continued to ask him eagerly, 'Tell us: what else have you seen?' he told them, 'In a little copse, a young faun played upon a flute to the dwellers in the woods, who danced to his piping.'

But one day when he had left the village, three mermaids who combed their green hair with a comb of gold rose up from the waves, and when they had departed, a centaur peeped at him from behind a hollow rock, and later, as he passed a little copse, he beheld a faun who played upon a pipe to the dwellers in the wood.

And that night, when the people of the village gathered at dusk, saying, 'Tell us: what have you seen today?' he answered them sadly, 'Today I have seen nothing.'

The Poet in Hell

Oscar Wilde's tales affected his listeners in a number of ways. Sometimes his audiences were stimulated, at others they were enchanted or seduced. The response of Lord Alfred Douglas, who probably heard more of Wilde's fables than anyone else, allows us to understand something of Wilde's power and his almost magical influence over his listeners. Douglas remarked that Wilde could cure anyone who was depressed or even physically ill simply by speaking to them for five minutes.

Many who heard him narrate attested to Wilde's almost miraculous powers in a similar fashion. The poet Ernest Dowson, for example, said that Wilde emanated such joy and vitality that, after a while, even a confirmed pessimist like himself could not but be infected by it. Frank Harris remembered that Wilde's talk had once cured him of a fever. Another friend, who had an agonizing toothache, listened to Wilde tell stories for over an hour, at the end of which he discovered that his toothache had gone.

The effect of the following story on Wilde's audience was as powerful if not quite as dramatic: after it was finished, his listeners remained motionless for some time. 'The Poet in Hell' grew spontaneously out of a discussion in a café during which Wilde claimed that, even if certain works of art are despised on earth, they may nevertheless be appreciated in the next world. Wilde may have told the fable in order to illustrate this theory – or perhaps he invented the theory as an introduction or an excuse for his tale.

Oscar Wilde, as drawn by James Edward Kelly in 1882.

I N HELL, AMONG ALL THE BRAVE COMPANY that is ever to be found there of lovers and fair ladies, and men of learning, and poets; amid all the ceaseless movement of doomed bodies, tossing and turning to be rid of the torment of their souls, one woman sat alone and smiled. She had the air of a listener, ever with lifted head and eyes raised, as though some voice from above were calling to her.

'Who is that woman?' enquired a newcomer, struck by the strange loveliness of her face, and by her enigmatic expression. 'The one with smooth, ivory limbs, and long hair falling down over her arms? Why is she the only soul whose eyes are ever looking upwards?'

He had not finished speaking before one made haste to answer, a man who carried in his hand a wreath of withered leaves.

'They say,' he told the newcomer, 'that on earth she was a great singer, with a voice like stars falling from a clear sky. When death came for her, God took her voice and cast it forth to the eternal echoes of the spheres, finding it too beautiful a thing to let die. And now she hears it with recognition, and remembering how once it was her own, she shares the pleasure which God takes in it. But do not speak a word to her, for she believes that she is in heaven.'

When the man bearing the wreath of withered leaves had finished and turned away, another man came up to the newcomer and said, 'No; that is not her story. It is this: on earth a poet made his song out of her beauty, so that her name became eternally wedded to his verse, and this verse still lives on the lips of men. Now, in hell, she lifts her head and can hear his praise of her sounded wherever language is spoken. That is her true story.'

'And the poet?' asked the newcomer. 'Did she love him well?'

'So little,' replied the other, 'that here in hell she passes him daily and does not recognize his face.'

'And he?'

The other laughed, and answered, 'It is he who just now told you that tale concerning her voice. In hell, he continues to tell the lies he used to tell about her when he was alive.'

The Counterfeit Coin

We have noted the effect of Oscar Wilde's talk on the sick and the depressed; it was equally efficacious with the bereaved and the dying. Whenever any of his friends suffered the loss of an acquaintance or relative, Wilde would demand to be admitted to their presence. Drawing up a chair beside his friends, he would begin by making them talk about their sorrow and end by making them laugh. 'He started,' remembered one, 'to tell all sorts of things, and I laughed though I thought that I should never laugh again.' It is also said that, as Wilde's friend Lord Lytton lay dying in Paris, he refused to see anyone, but asked Wilde to come to his bedside to tell him tales.

Reports such as these suggest something of Wilde's power as a talker; they are also a testimony to his incredible range. Although every story he told is suffused with his wit and lightness of touch, they frequently reduced people to tears. The following is typical of one of Wilde's pathetic tales as it also contains elements of fantasy and comedy. One version of the story grew out of a discussion in which Wilde maintained that those who have either love or genius are condemned to search in vain for someone with whom to share these gifts.

Wilde frequently invented impromptu stories about coins that were handed to him by members of his audience. After one such story, narrated during his final years in Paris, which concerned a king, a coin and a beggar, he is said to have remarked, 'I have been a king; now I will be a beggar.' He also told a variation of 'The Counterfeit Coin' in which the poor man who discovers the worthless coin challenges the king whose head it bears to a fight.

ONCE THERE WAS A VERY POOR MAN who wandered the highways of his country in search of whatever employment he could find along the way. One day on his journey he discovered by the roadside a golden coin on which there was the face of an unknown king.

'What luck!' cried the man, when he saw the golden coin glimmering in the sunlight. 'It is so long since I last ate a meal.' And so, proudly caressing the golden coin in his pocket, the poor man entered the nearest inn. Sitting down at a wooden table, he ordered as much as he could eat.

When the dishes and the glasses had been cleared away, the man brought out the golden coin with a flourish and threw it down on the table in order to settle his bill. But, on looking at the golden coin, the innkeeper frowned at the poor man and said, 'This golden coin is a counterfeit coin and the king whose face it bears is a counterfeit king.'

On hearing these words, the poor man replied, 'Alas: I have no other golden coin in all the world, but I will find employment hard by here and, after a time, I will surely earn that which I owe.'

After labouring twice as hard as usual for many days, the poor man was true to his word and paid the innkeeper's bill. Having paid the bill, the poor man gathered all of his clothes together in a bundle and took in his hand a long, wooden staff. Then, going forth from that place, he set out to discover the land in which he would be able to use his golden coin.

Working wherever he could along the way, the poor man wandered throughout the world. Through lands that were parched with heat he travelled, and through lands where the mountains were covered with snow. But never did he find the land for which he sought, and never did he see the face of the king. For although on his journey he passed through many kingdoms, he could not find the kingdom in which the king on the golden coin reigned.

And, whenever he came to a new city, the poor man would show his golden coin to the crowds of people who gathered around him and the people would look at it and say, 'Your golden coin is a counterfeit coin and the king whose face it bears is a counterfeit king.' But the poor man said to them, 'As the face of the king is a golden face, I am sure that he is reigning somewhere.'

And whenever the man went forth from each new city, the laughter of the people would follow him. But as he set his face to the sun and journeyed, the man was full of joy and, wherever he wandered, he would sing. For in his pocket he could feel the golden coin, and in his heart he felt hope.

On and on the poor man travelled, until at length he came to a great river and sat down wearily on its bank. It was evening, and in the dusky twilight he could see a boatman sitting close by him whose face was wizened and whose body was black. After hailing the boatman, the poor man asked him for a passage across the river. In return, he offered the boatman his golden coin. To the poor man's amazement, the boatman accepted it and led him down to the boat.

But as soon as the poor man and the boatman sat down in the boat, it began to sink under their weight. Into the darkening waters it sank, and the poor man's heart trembled with fear; into the swirling waters it sank and the poor man looked across at the boatman. And there, silhouetted in the gold of the dying sun, he beheld the face of the king on the golden coin, the king for whom he had searched throughout the world.

And with a smile of supreme contentment, knowing that he was leaving for a land from which there would be no return, the poor man, having finally parted with the golden coin, let the darkening waters flood over him.

Our Lady of Sorrows

It is likely that Wilde told the following tale during his triumphant visit to Paris in 1891 where, from the end of October to late December, he spoke every day for several hours at a time at dinners, lunches and in cafés. According to one French newspaper, he scattered tales around him as Buckingham had scattered jewels at the French court.

The event of the 1891 Paris season, Wilde soon became known as 'the poet who tells fantastic tales'. It is clear that, with his spoken stories, he seduced and conquered the capital. At several dinners he is said to have radiated light; at a gathering hosted by society figure Princess Ouroussoff, one guest screamed when she thought she saw a halo around his head.

Wilde's behaviour at a particular lunch in Paris was recorded in detail. Arriving an hour late, he asked for all the shutters to be closed, the candles to be lit, and the mauve cloth to be removed from the table. Then, somewhat arrogantly, he dominated the conversation with a rather macabre account of the various morgues he had visited in the capitals of the world. But for once he had misjudged his audience: no one wished to be shocked.

Over coffee, however, Wilde not only redeemed himself, but convinced his listeners that they were witnessing something close to a sacrament or miracle. 'He intoxicated us with his lyricism,' recalled one; 'his speech sounded like a hymn.' In a drawing room in the middle of noisy Paris, guests wept openly to think, as one of them remarked, that words could achieve such splendour.

Wilde in 1889. 'He lived,' wrote W. B. Yeats at
this time, 'in the enjoyment of his own invention.'

B Y THE SILVER MARGIN OF THE SICILIAN SEA there once stood a little shrine dedicated to Our Lady of Sorrows. And the fisher folk of that place worshipped her, bringing gilded apples and gilded shells, that their fishing might be prosperous, for her image was very ancient and often wrought miracles.

One midsummer eve, the setting sun smote the face of the goddess and, opening her eyes, she stretched forth her hands to unfasten the clasp of her mantle, whereon the seven daggers of the seven griefs, which once had pierced her heart, were wrought. Then, from her brow she removed her veil, and, white and naked, she arose and left her shrine.

And lo! as she passed the silver margin of the sea, nereids appeared among the waves, and eager Tritons blew upon their polished conches to greet her. From forests and fields came dryads and hoofed fauns, and from the caverned hills came centaurs bearing gifts. And Eros, her son, with scarlet wings aflame flew to embrace his mother. And all rejoiced that Beauty had once more returned to the waiting earth.

All night long there was high revelry. The sea nymphs sang and the centaurs danced till dawn, when the cock crew thrice. Then the goddess waxed very pale and, breaking from her worshippers, she moved towards the little shrine which stood by the margin of the sea.

In vain the fauns and dryads entreated her to stay, but she heeded them not and wrapped again the mantle of grief about her marble limbs. The centaurs wept and so did the Tritons, but she heeded not their tears and put the veil of mourning on her brow.

And when Eros besought her not to leave him, she bent down to him and said, 'I must again return to the place from whence I came, for you must know that I have another Son and He has suffered greatly!'

The Man Who Could Only
Think in Bronze

Henri de Régnier, the critic who heard Wilde narrate on a number of occasions in Paris, made many perceptive comments about his stories. He said that they were the perfect medium for the expression of Wilde's particular genius as they allowed him to articulate his paradoxical, ambiguous and contradictory thought. He also noted two of the ways in which Wilde kept the meaning of his tales indeterminate: he refused to explain any of them to listeners who asked him for an Aesopian 'moral'; he also altered the introductions or conclusions to the stories every time he told them.

'The Man Who Could Only Think in Bronze' illustrates the second of these habits. This particular version of the fable, narrated to André Gide, tells the story of a sculptor who, having melted down a bronze statue that symbolizes endless sorrow, makes from the metal a statue that symbolizes joy.

However, when Wilde later referred to the fable in *De Profundis*, he deliberately inverted its meaning. The man in the story no longer transforms the statue of sorrow into the statue of joy, but instead takes the statue of joy and fashions from it a statue of sorrow. This curious inversion is a wonderful demonstration of Wilde's theory that a truth in art is one whose opposite is also true. It should teach us to be very careful in affixing definitive meanings to any of his works, which always aim at complex beauty rather than at simple 'truth'.

THERE WAS ONCE A MAN WHO COULD only think in bronze. And one day he had an idea. It was the idea of the Joy that Dwells in the Moment, and the man felt compelled to express the idea. But all the bronze in the world had been used up, and though he searched everywhere, he could not find a single piece. And the man thought that he would go mad if he did not give expression to his idea.

Then he remembered the piece of bronze with which he had fashioned a statue on the tomb of his wife. On the tomb of his wife he had set the statue, for she was the only woman he had ever loved. It was the statue of Endless Sorrow, the Sorrow that Dwells in All Things. And the man thought that he would go mad if he did not give expression to his idea.

So he stood before the statue of Endless Sorrow, the Sorrow that Dwells in All Things. And, taking the statue, he smashed it and then melted it down in a fire. And with the bronze of the statue of Endless Sorrow he fashioned the statue of Joy, the Joy that Dwells in the Moment.

The Story of the Man Who Sold His Soul

Whenever Wilde was in Paris he narrated his fables in his colourful and deliberate French, which was as studied and as poetical as his English. He delighted in archaisms, chose words for their etymological value and beautiful sounds, such as those ending in -*âtre*, and French colour words as often as he could. While narrating, he would pause, ostensibly to search for the right word, but in fact to intensify the dramatic effect of his tale. One friend remarked that Wilde's spoken French was as lyrical and as exotic as the French he used for *Salome*; another compared his sentences to 'jewel-studded brocades'.

Although the following story dates from a period long after 1891, it is placed here because it is similar to Wilde's other fables. 'This is one,' he announced to the friends who sat around him, 'that has only just occurred to me, and I am not quite sure yet what the end of it will be. But it is there, waiting. You and I will listen to the story together, as I tell it for the first time.'

Despite the decorative form of the tale and the elaborate modulations of the voice with which he told it, Wilde seemed to be greatly moved as he narrated the story.

A CERTAIN TRAVELLER WAS PASSING THROUGH a great city when he saw a man sitting by the roadside upon whose countenance there was a grief he could not fathom. The traveller went over to the man and asked, 'What is this grief which you carry before the eyes of men, so grievous it cannot be hidden, yet so deep it cannot be read?'

The man answered him and said, 'It is not I who grieve so greatly; it is my soul, which I would send away from me. For my soul hindereth me from having my desires and I am weary of it. And therefore is my soul more sorrowful than death: it hates me, and I hate it.'

Then the traveller said, 'If you will sell your soul to me, you can be well rid of it.'

The man answered, 'But, how can I sell you my soul?'

'You have but to agree to sell me your soul at its true price,' replied the traveller. 'Then, when I bid it, it will come to me. Every soul has its true price, and for neither more nor less can it be sold.'

Then the man said, 'At what price shall I sell you this worthless thing, my soul?' The traveller answered: 'When a man first sells his own soul, he is like that other betrayer; therefore its price should be thirty pieces of silver. But after that, if it passes to other hands, its value becomes small, for to others the souls of their fellow men are worth but little.'

So for thirty pieces of silver the man sold his soul, and it entered inside the traveller and he departed. And after a time the man, having no soul, found that he could do no sin. For though he stretched out his arms wide to sin, sin would not come towards him. 'You have no soul,' said sin as it passed him by. 'Wherefore should

I come to you? For I have no profit in a man that has no soul.'

Then the man without a soul began to despair, for though his heart longed for wickedness, it remained pure; and though his hands touched what was foul, they remained clean. And when he desired to dip his fingers into the fire, they remained as cold as ice. Therefore a longing to recover his soul took hold of the man, and he wandered throughout the world in search of the traveller to whom he had sold it, that he might buy it back again and once more taste sin in his own body.

At length the man came upon the traveller and he asked him if he could buy back his soul. Hearing his request the traveller laughed and said, 'After a while your soul wearied me and I sold it to a Jew for a smaller sum than I paid you for it.' 'Ah!' cried the man. 'If you had come to me I would have paid you more.' The traveller answered, 'You could not have done that. A soul cannot be sold but at its true price, and your soul came to be of small value in my keeping.'

And so, parting from the traveller, the man wandered once more throughout the world in search of his lost soul. One day, when he came to a new city, he sat down in the marketplace to rest. After a time, a woman in a robe of green and silver came over to where he was sitting and asked him why he looked so sad. 'I am sad,' the man answered, 'because I have no soul, and over the whole world have I wandered in search of it.'

Then the woman said, 'Only the other night I bought a soul that had passed through so many hands that it had become almost worthless, and it is so poor a thing that I will gladly part with it. Yet

I bought it for a mere song; and a soul cannot be sold but at its true price. How, then, shall I be able to sell it again – for what is worth less than a song? And it was but a light song that I sang over a cup of wine to the man who sold it to me.'

When the man heard this, he cried, 'It is my own soul! Sell it to me, and I will give you all that I possess!'

'Alas!' said the woman. 'I did but pay for it with a song, and I cannot sell it again but at its true price. How then can I be rid of it, though it cries out and beseeches me piteously to set it free?'

The man without a soul laid his head to the woman's breast, and heard within it the captive soul crying to be set free, and to return to the body it had lost. 'Surely,' he said, 'it is my own soul! If you sell it to me I will give you my body, for it is worth less than a song from your lips.'

So, for the price of his body, the woman sold the man the soul that cried out to be set free. But as soon as he received the soul, the man rose up aghast and a cry of wild despair broke from his lips, 'What have you done?' he shouted. 'What is this foul thing that has possession of me? For this soul that you have given me is not *my* soul!'

Then the woman laughed and said, 'Before you sold your soul into captivity, it was a free soul in a free body; can you not recognize it now that it comes to you from the traffic of the slave-market? Indeed, your soul seems to have the greater charity, for it recognizes you and returns to you, though you have sold your body miserably into bondage!'

And thus it was that the man had to buy back, at the cost of his body, the soul that he had sold for thirty pieces of silver.

The Mirror of Narcissus

The effect of Wilde's fables on his listeners was sometimes of a 'Socratic' nature: it seemed to wake them up or force them to examine their lives or their vision of the world in a completely new way. Indeed, many of those who met Oscar Wilde were transformed by his conversation and sat 'open-mouthed and wondering' like Dorian Gray as he listened to Lord Henry Wotton. This was certainly the case with Wilde's young 'disciple', André Gide, who could only stare distractedly into his plate whenever Wilde began a tale. After having listened to him on one occasion, Gide wrote in his journal the single word 'WILDE'. Later he would remark, 'After Wilde, I hardly seem to exist.'

Gide heard many of Wilde's finest stories as they walked between restaurants or cafés, or when they spoke together in the corner of crowded salons. According to Gide, although Wilde hardly ceased narrating to his fellow guests throughout a lunch or dinner, he saved his best stories for small groups of his friends or even for an audience of one. Thus, during the elaborate discourses that were to undermine Gide's already wavering belief in Protestantism and conventional morality, Wilde told him 'The Disciple' (*see* pages 171 and 182).

The following version of the fable, which might be called 'The Mirror of Narcissus', also dates from the 1890s. When Wilde narrated the fable on one occasion, he introduced it with the following words: 'You listen with your eyes… that is why I will tell you this story.'

WHEN NARCISSUS DIED, the flowers of the field were stricken with grief, and begged the river for drops of water that they might mourn for him. 'If all my drops of water were tears,' replied the river, 'I should not have enough to weep for Narcissus. I loved him.'

'How could you help loving Narcissus?' said the flowers. 'He was so beautiful.'

'Was he beautiful?' asked the river.

'Who should know that better than yourself?' said the flowers. 'For every day, lying on your bank, he mirrored his beauty in your waters.'

'But I loved him,' murmured the river, 'because, when he leaned over me, I saw the reflection of my own beauty in his eyes.'

Wilde in 1892, as portrayed
in the Illustrated Sporting
and Dramatic News.

BIBLICAL TALES

*'To my words they durst add
nothing, and my speech
dropped upon them.'*

JOB 29:22 (WILDE'S EPITAPH)

The Thirty Pieces of Silver

Oscar Wilde was fascinated by the Bible. 'When I think,' he remarked, 'of all the harm that book has done, I despair of ever writing anything to equal it.' He had his own copy of the King James Bible covered in a luxurious green morocco binding and, after quoting long passages from it to friends, he would exclaim, 'How beautifully artistic these stories are!' The Bible inspired *Salome* and most of the plays he planned to write in his final years; its stately rhythms and cadences also had a profound influence on his style.

Yet Wilde was not content simply to employ the stylistic effects of the Bible; he wanted, in both his spoken and his written works, to rewrite it. He endeavoured to do this firstly by 'completing' what he thought of as the 'unfinished' tales of the Bible. Whenever he read stories such as those of Salomé, Jezebel or Moses, he always felt that certain details were missing and that it was his duty to recover them by an act of the imagination.

Wilde also 'rewrote' biblical tales by adding his own idiosyncratic gloss to them in order to invert their orthodox meaning. Thus, he would tell André Gide that Jesus did not love his mother because she was a virgin, or that Judas betrayed Christ because 'Each man kills the thing he loves.' The following story is a classic example of one of Wilde's ingenious 'misreadings'; when he told it, he repeated the version we find in Matthew until he reached the verse in which Judas hangs himself. At that point, he added the conversation between Judas and some of the other disciples.

AFTER HANDING OVER CHRIST to the chief priests, Judas cast down the thirty pieces of silver in the temple and went forth into the field to hang himself. Along the way, some of the disciples happened upon him and, seeing his torment and understanding his dark purpose, they asked him the cause of his woe.

And Judas answered them and said, 'Nay, but these chief priests are wretched and evil! They offered me ten pieces of silver to deliver Christ over to them.'

Then the disciples asked him, 'And did you agree to this?'

'Of course, I refused. But these chief priests are evil! For they then offered me twenty pieces of silver to deliver Christ over to them.'

'And,' the disciples asked him again, 'did you agree to this?'

'Of course, I refused. But they are merciless people! They then offered me thirty pieces of silver to deliver Christ over to them.'

'And,' the disciples asked Judas a third time, 'did you agree to this?'

'Alas,' Judas replied, 'I did.'

'Ah!' the disciples looked at him and said, 'now we understand why you have decided to hang yourself, for you have betrayed the innocent blood of Christ, and the sin you have committed deserves a punishment worse than death.'

'Oh no,' replied Judas. 'That is not the reason. I am going to the field to hang myself because the thirty pieces of silver the chief priests gave me were counterfeit.'

The Martyrdom of the Lovers

Wilde told the following story on one of his many visits to Oxford. The undergraduates of 'either university' constituted, perhaps, his ideal audience. They were, he said, 'so Greek and gracious and uneducated'; they also worshipped him uncritically as their 'divinity'. On many occasions Wilde would sit up all night, enthroned in the middle of a group of 'disciples', talking with them like a character from his own Platonic dialogues, just as he had done as an undergraduate at Magdalen.

The comments of two young men suggest something of the enchantment his talk held. 'I found him delightful,' wrote the poet Lionel Johnson of New College. 'He discoursed, with infinite flippancy, of everyone. Laughed at Pater and consumed all of my cigarettes. I am in love with him.' Another young poet said that, after having listened to Wilde, had the great man asked him to commit murder, he would have done so without a moment's hesitation.

Wilde told 'The Martyrdom of the Lovers' on an evening that was typical of many he spent at Oxford: he was guest of honour at a dinner given by Lord Alfred Douglas in his rooms in the High Street. Between each course, Wilde told jokes and passed around gold-tipped cigarettes. At the end of dinner, someone said, 'Oscar, do tell us a story.' To this Wilde replied in characteristic fashion with the question, 'And what, my dear boy, am I to tell you about?' On being offered 'The Early Church' as a subject, he shot out his great cuffs, looked round at his audience and began the following tale.

I N THE DAYS WHEN Christianity was beginning to convert the citizens of Rome, some of the rich patricians became interested in the strange and ascetic new creed. Among those who saw its terrible beauty was a girl called Lydia, who came from a great and ancient house. Her hair was gold, her body as pale as ivory and she was as fair as any young maiden in Rome. In her rich and colourful garments she went daily to the mean and dirty quarters where the small community of earnest Christians dwelt, and daily her fascination for the faith increased. At length, against the advice of all those who knew her, she decided to accept the baptism of Christ.

Now, during this time, Lydia had attracted the attention of the most handsome young patrician in Rome. But though Metellus's love for her burnt fiercely within his breast, he was unable to share her enthusiasm for the new faith. When she told him of her decision to become a Christian, he tried in vain to dissuade her from what seemed to him to be a form of social suicide.

Then one day Metellus came to Lydia, and, kneeling before her, he begged her to forsake her faith and to come away with him to be his bride. 'For love,' he said to her, 'is better than religion, and wiser than all the doctrines in the world.' But although Lydia's love was as intense as that of Metellus, her love for Christ was even stronger still. And so, with tears in her eyes, she told him that they could never marry unless he embraced the new faith.

Driven on by his flame-coloured love, Metellus at length consented to go with Lydia to hear what the Christians had to say.

When Metellus heard them, he was unmoved by their words, and indeed the whole thing seemed to him to be very foolish and unnecessary. But his love for Lydia burnt so fiercely that – seeing no other way of marrying her – he, too, decided to accept the baptism of Christ.

And so, for a while, they were happy together. But, before long, the activities of the Christians came to the attention of the cruel emperor, and a terrible persecution began. Along with their fellow believers, Lydia and Metellus were taken from their mean dwelling, hurled into prison and loaded down with heavy chains.

In the solitude and darkness of her cell, Lydia began to regret all that she had done. 'Perhaps, after all,' she said to herself, 'the whole story of Christ is false; certainly, the old gods were more indulgent and easier to please. How could I have been so foolish?'

And in the solitude and darkness of his cell Metellus thought, 'I knew from the first that all this ridiculous talk could only lead to trouble, and now what are we to do?'

Then, at length, the day arrived when each of them was told that they would be thrown to the wild beasts in the Great Circus before all the people of Rome unless they publicly renounced their faith.

Terror and anguish filled their hearts, but alone in her cell Lydia said to herself, 'I have brought all this upon myself and my dear Metellus. What am I to do? If I now renounce Christ, Metellus, who believes so fervently, will die despising me and that I could not bear.'

And alone in his cell Metellus said to himself, 'What a terrible business this is! For though I do not care about Christ or His absurd doctrine, if I renounce him now, my dear Lydia, whose belief in her own faith and in mine is as firm as a rock, will think me a coward and die despising me, and that I could not bear.'

And so when the appointed day came, Lydia and Metellus were taken from their cells and thrown to the wild beasts in the Circus before all the people of Rome.

And thus it was that they died for a faith in which they did not believe.

The Raising of Lazarus

Had the author Ernest Renan not already written the 'fifth gospel' of Christ in the mid-nineteenth century, Wilde would almost certainly have attempted it. It is clear that this was one of his ambitions; he wanted, he remarked to one friend, to write 'the Epic of the Cross, the *Iliad* of Christianity… [to delineate] the pure gift of Christianity as it was taught by Christ – free from the accretions of centuries of cant… to reclothe [Christ's] Sacrifice in new and burning words'.

Many of the stories in this section are, along with *De Profundis* and *The Soul of Man Under Socialism* (1891), fragments of this vast project. They offer us, in 'new and burning words', a Christ whose life is 'the most wonderful of poems', a Christ who, with sublime paradoxes and subtle parables not unlike Wilde's own, preached a creed of individualism, tolerance and joy. It is interesting to note that Wilde referred to the Gospels as the 'four prose poems' about Christ. This comment prompts us to read his own prose poems and biblical tales as extracts of his 'fifth gospel'.

The following story, told to André Gide, certainly reads like a set of verses from that 'fifth gospel'; it is an audacious misreading of John's account of the raising of Lazarus from the dead.

A ND AFTER JESUS HAD COME TO THE PLACE where the dead man was lain, He cried out with a loud voice, 'Lazarus, come forth.' And he that was dead came forth.

And, at length, when they had loosed him from the grave clothes that had lately bound him, Lazarus did not fall down at the feet of the One who had awoken him, but remained in silence and apart.

And Jesus drew nigh to where he was standing and spoke to him in a whisper and said, 'You who have been dead for four days and are now come unto us again, tell me: what is there beyond the shadows of the grave?'

Lazarus looked at Jesus reproachfully and said, 'Nay, but why have you spoken falsely to me and why do you persist in telling these lies about the wonder of heaven and of the glory of the eternal God? For know this, Rabbi: there is nothing after death and he who is dead, is dead indeed.'

When he heard this, Jesus raised a finger to His lips, and with an imploring look He said:

'I know. But don't tell anyone.'

The Shameful Death of Pope John XXII

Many of Wilde's disciples first met him when he visited Oxford or Cambridge. During these triumphant visits, nightly dinners were given in his honour. At one of these dinners, in rooms overlooking Saint Giles in Oxford, Wilde went out on to the balcony with one or two friends. Some of the passers-by in the street below recognized him and, much to his displeasure, started shouting his name. On hearing the uproar, Wilde's young friends immediately rushed out to disperse the crowd and to 'defend Wilde's honour'.

'You are magnificent,' Wilde exclaimed when they returned. 'You are giants – giants with souls.' As a reward for their efforts he agreed to tell them the following story, which he began when they had all resumed their seats.

'A little while ago,' Wilde said by way of a characteristic introduction, 'I was browsing in the library of a country house. I happened to pick out a musty, calf-bound volume of ancient European history… I opened it at random and my eye caught the sentence, "In that year Pope John XXII died a shameful death." This intrigued me (but, alas, I was unable to discover any information concerning the Pope's death in the library or at the British Museum) so I decided to discover the truth in the only way in which truth can be discovered – by evolving it from [my] inner consciousness.

'This process was difficult… but in the silence of the night the truth was finally delivered to me. It was this… '

*Wilde with Lord Alfred Douglas at Oxford, where the
former enchanted and thoroughly demoralized undergraduates.*

T HE AGED POPE, who had for a long time been little more than a living corpse, finally passed away. During his protracted illness, intrigue had been rife in Rome and the College of Cardinals had been torn by bitter faction. Every possible candidate had a party opposed to him and none of them could unite the Cardinals in agreement. And so, after the Pope had died, the Cardinals decided to make a compromise by appointing a neutral and completely unknown figure as the new Pope.

While they were discussing whom to appoint, one of the Cardinals suggested the young priest of a little country church that lay a few miles away from Rome. As he was intelligent, remarkably handsome, little over twenty years of age and as he had absolutely no connection at all with any of the warring factions in Rome, they decided to elect him. And so, summoned to the Vatican, the young priest was duly appointed Pope with all the elaborate ceremonies that attend such an occasion. He took as his name Pope John XXII.

Now, in those days, the Pope did not live a secluded life within the walls of the Vatican, but mixed freely in the society of Rome and tasted of all its delightful pleasures. As the hot blood of youth ran freely in his veins, and as he frequently met the most beautiful women of the capital, it is little wonder that Pope John should fall passionately in love.

The lady who captured his heart was the young wife of an elderly Roman nobleman. Her hair was as dark as the hyacinth blossom and her lips were as red as the rose. At first the lady rejected the addresses of the charming and youthful Pope, but, after a time, she was won over and a great love sprang up between them. First they loved with the love that dies, the love of the soul for the soul, and then they loved with the love that never dies, the love of the body for the body. But in Rome itself, their opportunities were few, for curious eyes were forever watching, and the tongue of scandal was never still. So they resolved to meet in some secluded spot far away from Rome.

As luck would have it, the young lady's husband owned a little villa with a beautiful orchard some miles outside of Rome. What meeting-place could be more perfect? The lady gave Pope John the key of a little postern gate that opened on to the orchard and they agreed on the day and the hour when they should meet.

Early on the appointed day Pope John arrayed himself in the colourful festival dress of a Roman nobleman, and, mounting his light-brown horse, he rode forth with exulting heart into the glorious countryside. As he passed through villages the peasants in their fields stopped their work to look at him, and when he rode through the forest the birds on the trees seemed to be singing of his love.

Now, after he had gone only a few miles, he saw in the distance the little church of which he had of late been the humble priest. Feeling an irresistible urge to visit the church, he decided to make a slight detour. After all, it was still very early in the day and he had plenty of time to spare.

He approached the little church and tethered his horse. Then a strange fancy took hold of him. He felt the curious desire to don the priest's purple vestments and to sit in the confessional as he had done so many times before. And so, on entering the empty church, he put on the vestments and sat down behind the grille. Sitting there he began to contemplate the strange vicissitudes of Fate: he thought of his extraordinary elevation to the Papacy and of the joys that awaited him later that day.

While he was pondering upon these matters, the door of the church suddenly flew open and a man with a face half-covered by a mask entered in a state of extreme anxiety. From his attire it was apparent that the man was an elderly Roman nobleman of some consequence. He came straight up to the confessional and grasped the rail with hands that betrayed his anguish.

'Father,' he said in a broken voice that was strangely familiar to the Pope, 'I have a question to ask of you.'

'Speak, my son,' said Pope John. 'What is it that you would know?'

'Is there,' asked the man, 'any sin so great that Christ cannot absolve it?'

'Nay, my son, there is no such sin,' answered the Pope. 'But tell me, what grievous sin has caused you to ask of me this?'

'I have as yet committed no such sin,' replied the man, 'but I am about to commit a sin so terrible that I do not think even Christ Himself could absolve me from it: for I am about to kill His Vicar on earth, Pope John XXII.'

Pope John replied in a voice which concealed his horror, 'Even from this sin could Christ absolve you.'

In great relief, the man rose and hurried out of the church. Then Pope John, slowly recovering from the feeling of terror the man's words had caused him, took off the purple vestments, mounted his horse and rode towards the orchard where his love awaited him. At length, he came to the little postern gate of the orchard and, opening it with the key his love had given him, Pope John entered inside.

And there, on the sunlit green turf in a clearing between trees that were covered with white blossoms, his lady stood with the radiant light of love in her eyes. A little cry broke from her lips and she ran towards him and threw herself into his open arms. But, as they stood in that first passionate embrace, a figure suddenly sprang from the shadows of the trees and drove a dagger deep into Pope John's back. A loud groan came from the mouth of the Pope as he fell to the ground.

The Pope looked up and, recognizing his assailant as the man he had spoken to in the church, he raised his hand and uttered the last words of the Absolution:

'*Quoad ego possum et tu eges, absolvo te.*'*

And so it was that Pope John XXII died a shameful death.

* 'As far as I can, and as far as you require it, I absolve you.'

The Temptation of the Hermit

Wilde told the following story at a dinner given by the American publisher J. M. Stoddart, at which Sir Arthur Conan Doyle was also present. Conan Doyle later remarked that, although Wilde towered above the other guests, he seemed to be interested in everything that was being said. This comment is not uncommon; by using the remarks of his listeners as the starting point for many of his tales, Wilde was able to make them feel that they, and only they, could have inspired him. 'The Temptation of the Hermit' is a fine example of this, as it was invented spontaneously during the course of the general conversation.

Over coffee and cigarettes, some of the other guests were discussing the cynical maxim that 'the good fortune of friends usually makes us discontented'. Wilde, who believed that 'anyone can sympathize with the sufferings of a friend, but it requires a very fine nature to sympathize with a friend's success', offered them this story as his contribution to the debate. It was typical of the man who thought that 'only the intellectually lost ever argue' to present his ideas on the subject in the form of story rather than as a dogmatic statement.

ONCE, WHILE THE DEVIL WAS CROSSING the Libyan desert, he came to a place where a number of small fiends were tormenting a holy hermit with images of the seven deadly sins. The willpower of the sainted man was too strong for them, and he easily shook off their evil suggestions.

Having watched the miserable failure of the demons, the devil stepped forward to give them a lesson. 'What you do is too crude,' he said. 'Permit me for one moment.' With that he whispered to the holy man, 'Your brother has just been made Bishop of Alexandria.' At once, a scowl of malignant jealousy clouded the serene face of the hermit.

'That,' explained the devil to his imps, 'is the sort of thing that I should recommend.'

Salome and the False Prophet

In Paris in 1891, the writer Gomez Carrillo heard Oscar Wilde narrate the following version of 'his' *Salome*. '"His" *Salome*, I say,' Carrillo later corrected himself. 'I am in error: for there were ten, no, a hundred *Salomes* that he imagined, that he began, that he abandoned.' Carrillo tells us that Wilde thought of writing *Salome* as a story, then as a poem and finally as a play; in fact, the play *Salome* was only written down as a result of a bizarre set of circumstances.

One afternoon, after he had been telling yet another version of the story in a café to a group of young writers, Wilde went back to his hotel and discovered a blank notebook in his room. It occurred to him that, as he had nothing else to do, he might as well write down the story as a play. After writing for a while he felt hungry and went out to get a sandwich at the Grand Café.

Having sat down and ordered, Wilde called the conductor of the orchestra over to him and said, 'I am writing a play about a woman dancing with bare feet in the blood of the man she has craved for and slain. I want you to play something in harmony with my thoughts.' The music that was played was, according to Wilde, so savage and so terrible that the other customers ceased to talk and looked at each other with blanched faces. Having listened to the music, Wilde went back to his hotel room to finish the play.

This story, which is almost as famous as the story of Coleridge writing *Kubla Khan*, tells us a great deal about the manner in

Salome, as illustrated by Aubrey Beardsley for Wilde's play of 1894.

which Wilde wrote down his works. Having created and recreated the stories endlessly at dinner tables, he set them down when the mood (or, in some cases, financial imperatives) forced him to do so.

Even though sceptics may question the literal truth of Wilde's account of *Salome*'s conception and delivery, it is impossible to deny that the form and even the content of the published play were dictated by circumstance and by Wilde's whimsical mood. Like all of Wilde's works, *Salome* was written out in great haste and with a ferocious energy while the mood in which it had been conceived remained with him. Wilde may have been exaggerating when he remarked of the notebook, 'If it had not been there, I should never have dreamed of doing it', but his comment has, at the very least, the value of a 'symbolic' truth.

I N THOSE DAYS WHEN John the Baptist's words had caused a great multitude to come to him to be baptized on the banks of the Jordan, he spoke out against Herod and said, 'It is not lawful for Herod to take Herodias for his wife, for she is the wife of his brother, Philip.'

Now, John's fame spread so far throughout the land that an impostor, thinking to share in his popularity, usurped his name and habit and began to preach to the multitude in his voice. And, while John fled to the mountains to escape the wrath of Herod, the impostor, thinking that the love of the multitude for his borrowed name would protect him, sought to extract golden coins from Herod in return for the promise of his silence. But Herod, who would not bargain with the impostor, sent forth his servants to lay hold of him. And, thinking him to be the prophet John, Herod had him bound in prison and loaded down with heavy chains.

Now, the nurse of the little Princess Salome, daughter of Herodias and Philip, was a woman of the same country as the prophet John. Often had she gone forth to the banks of the Jordan to listen to the words of the Baptist and, hearing his words, she had been greatly moved. And she was one of the few who understood that John's name and habit had been usurped by the impostor, and she had knowledge of the error that Herod had made. Ever did she speak to her young mistress of the prophet and, after a time, she told her of Herod's mistake.

When the anniversary of his birthday came and Herod made supper with his lords and high captains, the little Princess Salome danced in front of his guests. Innocent and chaste she was as she whirled around before them, joyful she became as she trembled all over in ecstasy. She wore a white muslin dress that was studded with pearls, and when her little naked feet moved on the carpet, they were like white doves. Seeing her dance, Herod swore unto her that whatsoever she should ask, that would he give her, even unto half of his kingdom.

Then Salome went forth to the place where her mother was sitting and she said to her, 'What shall I ask?' Herodias answered, 'The head of John the Baptist,' for she had a quarrel against him and would have had him killed long before. Then Salome went to the place where the nurse was sitting and said to her, 'What shall I ask?' And the nurse, thinking to punish the impostor, answered, 'The head of John the Baptist.' And so, more for the sake of her nurse than for her mother, the Princess Salome came in straightaway with haste before Herod and said: 'I would that they presently bring me on a silver charger, the head of John the Baptist.'

Now Herod, knowing that John was a wise man and a just, heard her and was afraid. Yet for his oath's sake, and for the sake of the guests gathered there, he sent for the executioner and commanded that the head be brought before her. When the executioner brought the bloody head on a silver charger to the Princess Salome, she turned her pale visage away in fear.

Then her mother let out a proud and haughty laugh, and looking down at the head on the silver charger, she said, 'I am well pleased with my daughter. For she has shut for ever the mouth that was always wont to hurl slanders at me.'

But later that same night, Herodias found that she could not sleep in her purple chamber and she went out onto the marble terrace that was bathed in the light of the pale-yellow moon. And there, rising up towards her from the mist of the marshes and the ditches full of shadows, she heard the voice of the one whom she had thought to have silenced, and his curses were more virulent than before.

Then Herodias waxed pale and went forth to the chamber of Herod who was sleeping deeply after the wine of the feast. 'Listen!' she cried. 'It is the voice of the one whom we thought dead and he is risen from the grave to torment us!'

And, hearing Herodias speak these words to one who had taken the place of her father, the Princess Salome sighed in her chamber with deep satisfaction – and turned over to sleep.

The Double Beheading

Wilde's imagination was so capacious that it seemed to contain every one of Salome's 'possible universes'. In his mind, Salome could be both a saint and a harlot, and every interpretation that was artistically realized was 'true' – even though it might contradict his previous version of the tale. In some accounts, the princess's lust and corruption are limitless; in others, she dances chastely before Herod with an air of resignation as though she is obeying a divine command. In one story attributed to Wilde, Salome drinks the water of the Jordan, which carries the soul of the dead Baptist; the soul, on entering her body, miraculously impregnates her. In another version Salome goes to France with Herodias, then dances on the frozen waters of the Rhône.

Wilde narrated the following version of *Salome* at the house of the writer Jean Lorrain, at a dinner with the Symbolist writer Marcel Schwob, novelist Anatole France and a few others. Lorrain, who was fascinated by Donatello's painting of the severed head of an unknown woman, had had a bust of the head made for him, which he placed in his dining room. On seeing it, Wilde immediately turned pale and exclaimed, 'Why, it is Salome! I swear to you it's true!' With his eyes fixed on the bust he then told the following story, which he claimed to have taken from a gospel that had been recently discovered in Nubia. Afterwards, Wilde's guests urged him to write it down, and it seems likely that, during his stay in Paris, he did begin and then discard a story entitled 'The Double Beheading'.

Wilde circa 1892. At about this time, he wrote to a
fellow author: 'We must make merry over a flagon of wine,
and invent new tales with which to charm the world.'

SHE WAS PRINCESS OF JUDEA and the niece of Salome, and she was identical to Salome in every way. As capricious and passionate as Salome was she, and she was as wilful and as fair.

Her lover was a young philosopher of the city of Rome who had been raised on the wisdom of the Greeks. Ever in his youth had he been surrounded by beauty, and ever had he been nourished on the honey and milk of Plato's words.

Now, when an apostle of Christ came to preach the new religion in Judea, the young philosopher laughed scornfully at his words. With ingenious argument, he refuted the new creed of pain and sorrow, and with impassioned lyricism he spoke of a faith based on the ardent worship of beauty and joy. Thinking to please her lover, the Princess of Judea gave the order to one of her black slaves to cut off the apostle's head. So, presently, on a golden charger, she brought the bleeding head before the young philosopher.

As the young philosopher gazed at the severed head on the golden charger he shuddered at its ugliness and at the violence that had been done. And, after a time, to revenge the discomfort she had caused him, he smiled a chill smile at the Princess and said, 'My darling, it would please me more if the head on this golden charger were your head!'

Hearing this, the Princess bit her lip, grew pale and went away without a word. Later that same evening, in accordance with her supreme order, the black slave who had slain the apostle cut off his royal mistress's head. At length, he brought it on a golden charger to the garden where the young philosopher lay reading from his book of Plato.

After gazing at the severed head of his lover for some time, the young philosopher turned away from it and murmured to himself, 'What is the reason for all of this bloodshed?'

And then he carried on reading as before.

The Decapitation of Saint Salome

Oscar Wilde's response to the 'official' version – or rather, versions – of *Salome* was entirely characteristic: he thought that, as the various biblical scribes had 'left out' several important details, it was his duty as an artist to finish the tale for them. Indeed, he maintained that it was the very incompleteness of the biblical accounts that had made it necessary for painters and artists to heap up dreams and visions at the feet of Salome over the centuries.

The following version of *Salome* uses the biblical narrative as little more than a starting point; after the opening lines, Wilde develops a tale in the manner of the *Lives of the Saints*. It was perhaps after the narration of this particular *Salome* that the writer Rémy de Gourmont criticized Wilde for inaccuracy and for infidelity to the historical 'truth'. 'What [Gourmont] told us was the truth of a professor,' Wilde later remarked. 'I prefer the other truth: my own, which is that of a dream. Between two truths, the falser is the truer.'

Like 'Salome and the False Prophet', 'The Decapitation of Saint Salome' was narrated at Jean Lorrain's house. According to Lorrain, the bust of the severed head, around the neck of which some congealed blood had been placed, again inspired Wilde. Pointing at the bust, Wilde tried to convince the other guests that it was not a plaster bust, but the severed head of Salome miraculously preserved over the centuries by ice. Jean Lorrain, Wilde went on, must have danced for Salome's head to avenge his namesake, John the Baptist. In an instant, these observations began to crystallize in Wilde's mind into the following tale.

WHEN HEROD SAW the Princess Salome kissing the mouth of the Baptist's severed head, he was wroth, and he wanted to command his guards to rush forward and crush her beneath their golden shields. But on hearing the supplication of his wife, Herodias, he contented himself with banishing the princess from his palace. And so Princess Salome set her face to the sun and journeyed through the desert. And there she lived on for many years, accursed and alone.

Then, after a time, when Jesus passed through the desert where she dwelt, she recognized the One whom the dead voice had prophesied and, seeing Him, she believed. But, thinking herself to be unworthy of His company, she would not follow Him. Instead, she set her face to the sun once more and journeyed on through the desert in order to spread his word. And whenever she passed through a village she preached the good news about Christ, and whenever she entered into a new city, she spoke to the crowds of his boundless love.

On and on she journeyed, across the rivers and the seas, and after she had passed through the deserts of fire, she came to the deserts of snow. One day, as she crossed a frozen lake, the ice cracked beneath her feet. As she plunged down into the freezing water, a sharp piece of ice cut into her neck and decapitated her instantly. And, in the very moment of her death, she cried out the names of Jesus and John. And all those who passed by the river saw, on the silver plate of frozen ice which had formed around her neck, the head of Princess Salome, glittering like a flower with a ruby stamen, above which there shone a halo of gold.

Saint Robert of Phillimore

Oscar Wilde was unmistakably and, at times, defiantly Irish. In Paris in 1891, he described himself to journalists as 'French by sympathy… Irish by race and the English have condemned me to speak the language of Shakespeare'.

Shaw and Yeats understood Wilde's Irishness. They saw that his entire life was an extravagant Celtic crusade against beer, the King James Bible, the seven deadly English virtues and the unimaginative Anglo-Saxon intellect. In their view, Wilde was an 'Irishman to the core' – and this fact is evident in many of his spoken tales.

When Wilde invented his stories, he was drawing upon the vast reservoir of Irish folk tales his father and mother had told him as a child. Many of his own stories were inspired by them. The following tale, for example, echoes the saints' lives that survive as part of Irish folklore, some of which Wilde's own mother collected in her book *Ancient Legends, Mystic Charms and Superstitions of Ireland* (1888).

'Saint Robert of Phillimore' was told as a gentle satire on the excessive religious zeal of Wilde's great friend Robert Ross, who had a house in Upper Phillimore Gardens in London. In one of his letters, Wilde refers to Ross's canonization: 'I shall now live,' he wrote, 'as the infamous Saint Oscar of Oxford, Poet and Martyr. My niche is just below that of the Blessed Saint Robert of Phillimore, Lover and Martyr – a saint known in the *Hagiographa* for his extraordinary power, not in resisting, but in supplying temptations to others. This he did in the solitude of great cities, to which he retired at the comparatively early age of eight.'

THERE WAS A CERTAIN SAINT who was called Saint Robert of Phillimore. Every night, while the sky was yet black, he would rise from his bed and, falling on his knees, pray to God that He, of His great bounty, would cause the sun to rise and make bright the earth. And always, when the sun rose, Saint Robert knelt again and thanked God that this miracle had been vouchsafed.

Now, one night, Saint Robert, wearied by the vast number of more than usually good deeds he had done that day, slept so soundly that when he awoke the sun had already risen, and the earth was already bright.

For a few minutes Saint Robert looked grave and troubled, but presently he fell down on his knees and thanked God that, despite the neglect of His servant, He had yet caused the sun to rise and make bright the earth.

The God Who Left His Temple

As well as being a famous eye surgeon, Wilde's father, Sir William Wilde, was one of the first folklorists of Ireland. Whenever a peasant was unable to afford Sir William's fee, he asked for payment in the form of a tale. Later he collected these tales in a volume entitled *Irish Popular Superstitions* (1852). After Sir William's death, Lady Wilde continued his work by publishing a further two books from the legends, superstitions and charms he had collected.

Wilde delighted in these tales and legends; they were a fundamental part of the landscape of his imagination. In fact, the very cadences and rhythms of the tales published by his parents can be heard in Wilde's own stories. The following tale echoes these rhythms; it is also similar to many of the 'religious' stories of Irish folklore in so far as it can be described, in Lady's Wilde's words, as 'an amalgam of Pagan myth and Christianity'.

Wilde told the tale at the house of the artist Charles Ricketts, who remembered him telling and retelling all of the stories that would be published later as *Poems in Prose*. In this story, Wilde seems to have combined two of his prose poems, 'The Master' and 'The Doer of Good'. He told it while discussing his adversary, the American painter James Whistler, whom he criticized for writing about art in the newspapers: 'Art,' he said, 'should always remain mysterious... Artists, like gods, must never leave their pedestals.' Then he laughed out loud and added, 'I must tell you this fantasy of mine: how a certain god left his temple out of compassion for the world.'

I N A STREET OF SIN, a god besought a harlot to leave her life of shame, but she heeded him not, and turning to one who wore roses in his hair, she kissed his painted lips. And the leper the god had cured of his sores followed her and became her lover.

The god then changed water into wine, but the wedding guests would not drink, for they knew that, being a god, he could not taste joy.

And when he put dust upon his flesh and crowned himself with thorns, they mocked at his wounds, and would not slay him, because a god cannot know sorrow.

The Best Story in the World

Yeats recognized the particularly oral and the specifically Irish nature of Wilde's genius. He understood that Wilde was a talker rather than a writer, in the conscientious and rather 'earnest' sense that Henry James or Charles Dickens were writers. Largely as a result of this perspective, Wilde emerges from Yeats's memoirs as a kind of ancient Irish bard who, by some miracle or glorious mistake, happened to be born into the late-Victorian world.

Yeats was in no doubt that Wilde's spoken works were superior to those he wrote down. Behind his spoken stories, Yeats said, Wilde put the whole force of his intellect; he only achieved greatness in his written works when they mirrored his speech. In later life, whenever Yeats read Wilde's works, he tried to imagine him in the act of telling them 'half-consciously watching that he might not bore by a repeated effect, some child or some little company of young painters or writers…' 'To enjoy [the stories],' he concluded, 'I must hear his voice once more, and listen once more to that incomparable talker.'

Yeats's response to the following fable was equally enthusiastic: he said it added something new to the imagination of the world. He introduced 'The Best Story in the World' with an interesting anecdote. One day, on asking a friend of Wilde's what the master storyteller had been doing of late, the man replied, 'Oh, he is very melancholy. He gets up about two in the afternoon, for he tries to sleep away as much of life as possible, and he has made up a story that he calls "The Best Story in the World" and says that he repeats it to himself after every meal and upon going to bed at night.'

CHRIST CAME FROM A WHITE PLAIN to a purple city, and as He passed through the first street, He heard voices overhead, and saw a young man lying drunk upon a window-sill. 'Why do you waste your soul in drunkenness?' He asked. And the young man answered, 'Lord, I was a leper and You healed me. What else can I do?'

A little further through the town He saw a young man following a harlot, and asked, 'Why do you dissolve your soul in debauchery?' And the young man answered, 'Lord, I was blind, and You healed me. What else can I do?'

At last, in the middle of the city, He saw an old man crouching, and weeping upon the ground, and when He asked why he wept, the old man answered, 'Lord, I was dead, and You raised me into life. What else can I do but weep?'

The Exasperation of Nero

Although he completed *The Ballad of Reading Gaol* (1898) and made some revisions to two of his plays, Oscar Wilde effectively ceased to write after his release from prison in 1897. On being asked what he intended to write, he would say that he was going to set down one of the plays from which he continually quoted, or develop one of his spoken stories into a full-length drama. At other times he mentioned projected essays on subjects such as 'The Defence of Drunkenness' or 'The Effect of the Colour Blue on Men' and poems such as 'Ballad of a Fisher Boy'.

Wilde never carried out any of these projects. In private he admitted that two years' hard labour had destroyed his vitality and power of concentration. 'The intense energy of creation,' he said, 'has been kicked out of me.' Other factors, such as loss of social position, the insults of his enemies and the slights of former friends no doubt contributed to the problem, and continual worries about money inevitably diminished what he called 'the joyous power on which art depends'.

Yet Wilde's talk was, according to his friends, better than ever. To his very last days, when he lavished his ingenious inventions on anyone who would listen to him (or who was willing to pay for his drinks), he simply could not stop telling his tales. The writer Vincent O'Sullivan was one of his best listeners in these years; he remembered the following tale about Nero. It was probably Wilde's imaginative attempt to explain Nero's decision to persecute the Christians.

YOU KNOW, NERO WAS OBLIGED to do something. They were making him look ridiculous. What he thought was this:

'Here everything was going on very well, when one day two incredible creatures arrived from somewhere in the provinces. They are called Peter and Paul, or some unheard-of names like that. Since they came here, life in Rome has become impossible. They gather crowds around them and block the traffic with their miracles. It really is intolerable. I, the Emperor, have no peace. When I get up in the morning and look out of the window, the first thing I see is a miracle going on in the back garden.'

A cartoon showing Wilde, in full flow, with the Lord Chamberlain, circa 1892.

A caricature of Wilde that appeared in Pick-Me-Up
*in 1894. 'The liar,' according to Wilde, 'at any rate recognizes
that recreation, not instruction, is the aim of conversation.'*

Jezebel

Wilde told the story of Jezebel on many occasions before his imprisonment. It is likely, however, that the idea of turning the tale into a play came to him while re-reading the Bible in Reading Gaol. Having read the account of Jezebel's appropriation of the vineyard of Naboth in I Kings 21, Wilde characteristically decided that something had been left out of the story. Apparently, in his play, Queen Jezebel would have been a quite different figure from the 'hussy' of the biblical legend.

Whenever he told the story, Wilde altered its title as well as its plot, sometimes referring to it as 'Ahab and Isabel', at other times calling it 'The Vineyard of Naboth'. After telling it to friends, he would remark that he had almost completed the play in his head. He also said that he intended the main part for the French actress Sarah Bernhardt.

No manuscript draft of the play survives, nor has one ever been known to exist. The following story dates from the early 1890s, and it seems to bear little relation to the play Wilde contemplated writing in his final years.

QUEEN JEZEBEL STOOD ON HER MARBLE TERRACE gazing out at the fair lands which lay around the palace Ahab the King had built. She was wrapped in a robe of woven gold, and long strands of emeralds coiled about her; they glittered and sparkled in the dusky twilight like green snakes at play. Her long white hands were circled with gems, and her blood-red hair hung in thick braids on either side of her pale face. In her splendour and in her deadly beauty, she looked like some marvellous idol.

She sighed a deep and heavy sigh, and Ahab the King said to her, 'Wherefore sighest thou, O Queen of Beauty? Is there anything in the heavens or on the earth thy soul desires? Hast thou not all that gold can buy and all that men can fashion with the labour of their hands? Yet if there is anything that thy soul desires, am I not here to give it to thee? For am I not thy slave, O Queen of Beauty, even though I be King of Syria?'

As one who is wearied with a great weariness and sick unto death with the satiety of fulfilled desires, in slow and languid accents the Queen answered Ahab the King, 'It is true, O King, that I have all that the earth can give: gems and gold and garments of Tyrian purple and woven silver – all these things are mine. And I have marble palaces filled with slaves and dancing girls, and rose gardens and palm trees and orange groves where the scent lies heavy at noon.

'And the camels travel ceaselessly across the wide desert, laden with perfumes and rare and costly materials and treasures for my delight. And every man on the earth is my slave, for I am almighty in my beauty. Even thou, Ahab, bow before me in the dust, and thou art King of Syria.

'But hard by the palace, there is a vineyard which belongs to another where the grass is green and the white doves fly; and therefore, O King, do I sigh.'

Ahab the King answered her and said, 'Sigh not, O Jezebel, Queen of Beauty, for surely thou shalt have the vineyard where the grass is green and where the white doves fly. For it is the vineyard of Naboth, friend of my bosom and my standard-bearer, who hath twice in battle saved my life.'

Then Ahab the King sent for Naboth.

Now Naboth was a youth of twenty years and, as he stood before the King, he was very fair to look upon. And Ahab the King put his hand on Naboth's mighty shoulder and spake unto him, saying, 'Naboth, the Queen doth desire thy vineyard. I will therefore cover it with gold pieces and precious gems, which thou shalt take in place of the land, or whatsoever else thou shalt appoint either in honours or in treasure, that shalt thou have. For the Queen doth desire thy vineyard, Naboth.'

But Naboth answered him and said, 'Nay, King. The Lord Himself forbid me that I should give the inheritance of my fathers unto any man. Nay, I may not part with it, O King, not even for all the treasure on the earth.'

Then Jezebel the Queen spoke to Ahab the King, and her voice was as low and soft as the sighing of the summer breeze at evening: 'Do not trouble him further, O King, for the vineyard shall not be taken from him. Suffer him to go in peace.'

Then Ahab went forth and likewise Naboth.

But later that day Jezebel sent for Naboth; and when Naboth stood before her, she said unto him, 'Come hither, Naboth, and seat thyself beside me on this throne of ivory and gold.'

But Naboth answered her and said, 'Nay, Queen, that may I not do, for the throne of ivory and gold is the throne of Ahab, King of Syria, and on it may no man sit beside thee, save only the King.'

Then the Queen said unto him, 'I am Jezebel, the Queen, and I command you to be seated.'

And Naboth sat beside her on the throne of ivory and gold.

Then the Queen said unto him, 'Here is a drinking cup carved out of a single amethyst. Drink from it, Naboth!'

But Naboth answered her and said, 'Nay, it is the drinking cup of Ahab, King of Syria, and from it should no man drink, save only the King.'

Then the Queen said unto him, 'I am Jezebel, the Queen, and I command you to drink.'

And Naboth drank from the drinking cup that was carved out of a single amethyst.

Then the Queen said unto him, 'I am very fair. There is none so fair on all the earth. Kiss me, Naboth!'

But Naboth answered her and said, 'Thou art the wife of Ahab, King of Syria, and no man may kiss thee, save only the King.'

Then the Queen said, 'I am Jezebel, the Queen, and I command you to kiss me.'

And the Queen twined her ivory arms around the neck of Naboth, so that he could not escape. Then she cried in a loud voice saying, 'Ahab! Ahab!'

And Ahab the King did hear her, and coming into the room he saw her lips on the lips of Naboth, and her ivory arms twined around his neck. Then, mad with rage, Ahab ran his spear through the body of Naboth, and Naboth fell down to the marble floor.

When Ahab the King saw the friend of his bosom lying in his blood, his wrath left him and his heart filled with remorse.

He cried out, 'O Naboth! Friend of my bosom and my standard-bearer, you who twice in battle have saved my life, have I indeed with these hands now killed thee, and is the blood upon them thy young heart's blood? Would that it were mine own, Naboth, and would that I were lying where thou art lying now!'

The grief of Ahab the King ate into his very soul and his moaning filled the air. But Jezebel the Queen smiled a strange, sweet smile and, in a voice which was as low and soft as the sighing of the summer breeze at evening said unto him:

'Nay, King, thy lamentations are foolish and thy tears are vain. Rather shouldst thou laugh. For now the vineyard where the grass is green and the white doves fly is mine own.'

The Miracle of the Stigmata

'The Miracle of the Stigmata' is an exemplary oral narrative, an ingenious adaptation of a traditional tale, which survives in a number of vastly different versions. Frank Harris adapted it as a short story. In his version, Paul, who comes to preach in Caesarea, converts a woman called Judith to the new faith. When Judith recounts Paul's words to Joshua, her husband, he becomes angry and insists that Paul has completely misunderstood Christ's message of love. On Paul's advice, Judith then leaves her husband to join the Christian community. Many years later, when she returns to her house to bury Joshua, she discovers the stigmata of Jesus on his hands. She then consults Paul, who interprets the stigmata as a sign that God has deliberately placed on the body of the sinful 'unbeliever' to show the world the glorious and triumphant truth of the Christian faith.

Wilde told the story in the early 1890s to his friend Adela Schuster. Yeats also recorded a shortened version. One day Wilde announced to him, 'I have been inventing a Christian heresy.' He then proceeded to tell Yeats a version of the tale that ends 'Once Saint Paul visited [Christ's] town, and He alone in the carpenters' quarter did not go to hear him preach. Henceforth the other carpenters noticed that, for some reason, He kept His hands covered.' Although these versions differ from each other, Jesus is always the only man on earth who understands the falsity of the new faith and the resurrection.

The following version of 'The Miracle of the Stigmata' was told in a café on Christmas night in 1899, almost exactly a year before Wilde died. As he spoke, he half-closed his red and swollen eyes.

WHEN JESUS WAS HANGING on the cross, there came to the soldiers a rich man of Arimathea, named Joseph. And Joseph bribed the soldiers with his money and made them take the sponge which they had dipped in bitter vinegar and soak it instead with a magical elixir that gave to the one who swallowed it the semblance of death. Then the soldiers put the sponge up to Jesus on the end of a long spear and He opened His mouth and drank of it.

After they had taken down the body of Jesus from the cross, and Joseph of Arimathea had lain Him in the sepulchre which was hewn out of the rock, Jesus's women, pretending that they had come to anoint Him with sweet spices, awoke their master from His deep slumber and freed Him from the tomb. Then, after travelling far from cruel and ungrateful Jerusalem, Jesus took refuge in an obscure country town. There He returned to His former trade as a carpenter, and the people marvelled much at his gift for fashioning crosses and cribs.

Now, after a time, the Apostle Paul came to preach in the town where Jesus was dwelling. Of all those in the brotherhood of the carpenters, only Jesus did not go to hear him: for He knew very well that Paul would distort His real message and that He would tell lies about the resurrection of His body.

When the other carpenters returned, they were filled with joy and they came to Jesus to tell him about the Saviour of the World. With tears in their eyes, they spoke of the Messiah who had been crucified by his own people, of the Christ whose hands and whose feet had been driven through with nails. On hearing these words, Jesus bowed His head in fear and hid His hands in the sleeves of His tunic. From that day forth, His fellow carpenters could not but notice that, for some unaccountable reason, He covered His hands at all times.

For many years made up of work and silence, Jesus lived on in the town surrounded by men whom Paul had converted. He was the only man in the whole of the world who knew the falseness of the new faith.

And, in the passing of time, when Jesus breathed His last and His companions came to bury Him, they discovered the wounds that were on His hands and His feet. Kneeling in astonishment beside Jesus' body, they worshipped it as the body of one who is a saint, and looking down at the stigmata they cried: 'Behold, our brother is a Saint of Christ! It is a miracle. It is a great miracle!'

Phil May's drawing of Wilde in 1893. 'All my life,' Wilde said, 'I have been looking for twelve men who did not believe in me... so far I have only found eleven.

Moses and Pharaoh

Long before his incarceration in 1895, Oscar Wilde spoke of writing the following story as a play, to which he gave the provisional title *Pharaoh*. It was in prison, however, that his ideas on the subject seem to have taken definite form. During an interview with a friend at Reading Jail, Wilde referred to the play, saying, 'The King is tremendous when he cries to Moses, "Praise be to thy God, O prophet, for He has slain my only enemy, my son!" But [in order to set it down] I must have books about Egypt full of names of beautiful things, rare and curious meat for the feast…'

Wilde's comments about *Pharaoh* are typical of the way in which he spoke of plays he intended to write. It was as though they already existed in their entirety in his mind and that, like a literary equivalent of Mozart, all he had to do was transcribe them. During a discussion with Robert Ross and a few others, Wilde alluded to his habit of quoting from unwritten yet 'finished' works. 'It is enough,' he remarked, 'that they actually exist; that I have been able, in my own mind, to give them the form which they demand… If I could write what I have been saying to you; if I could hope to interest others as I seem to have interested you, I would; but the world will not listen to me now…'

Wilde went on telling the story of *Pharaoh* right up to the end of his life, including a version he referred to as 'Moses and Pharaoh' that was told to the actor Edouard de Max. It is possible that the story de Max heard was similar to the following version, which dates from the same period.

AND SO IT CAME TO PASS in the process of time that the old Pharaoh of Egypt died. And his daughter, who had saved the infant Moses in the ark of bulrushes daubed with pitch and slime from the river full of crocodiles, became the wife of her own brother, the new Pharaoh of Egypt, in accordance with the sacred laws of the land.

And Moses and Aaron came before the new Pharaoh to deliver unto him the words of the Lord. And, just as the Lord had commanded him, Moses cast down his rod in front of Pharaoh, and lo! it rose up from the ground and became a serpent with scales of emerald. And when Moses stretched forth the hand that had been the scourge of all Egypt, it became covered with leprosy.

Now, at this time, it had come to pass that the Lord smote all the firstborn in the land of Egypt, from the firstborn of the Pharaoh that sat on his throne unto the firstborn of the captive that was in the dungeon, and all the firstborn of the cattle.

And the Queen, lamenting the death of her son – the firstborn of Pharaoh – entered the place where Moses and Aaron stood before Pharaoh. Recognizing Moses, the scourge of all Egypt, she came forward and said unto him, 'Are you not the infant I saved from the river that is full of crocodiles when I came unto you in your little ark of bulrushes daubed with pitch and slime? In that time, my departed father did reign over this house and he was ruler over all of the land. But he is dead, and now, in accordance with our sacred law, my brother and lord has taken me for his wife. And it is he, who was once the friend of your youth – he, who was even as your elder brother – whom you now do so mightily offend and with whom you deal so proudly.'

When Moses heard her, he sighed deeply and answered her and said, 'I did only as the Eternal Lord commanded. All things did I according to His word.'

And Pharaoh drew nigh to Moses and said unto him, 'And who is the Eternal Lord, that I should obey His voice to let the people of Israel go? I know not the Eternal Lord, but, of a truth, I know you, Moses, and there has been great affliction among my people and great affliction in this house since last you came before me. And have you now come unto us again that we may cry further, and that you may behold the lamentation of my sister and Queen?'

And, as the Queen stood lamenting before him, Moses came unto her as one who would offer consolation, but she thrust him away and said, 'I saved you when you were yet an infant from the river that is full of crocodiles and now, at your command and by your own hand, have you not taken my own infant away from me? And has it not then come to pass that, in saving you, I have killed my own firstborn? Yea, just as I gave him life even so did I take it away. Of this, and of this alone am I certain, for all of us end by killing the thing we love. And now may I be cursed with endless affliction. Put upon me the leprosy that appears and hides itself even as you command it. Moses, take thy rod of dead wood and cast it down to the earth so that the serpent which springs out of it may rise up in the air and bite me.'

Then Moses answered her and said, 'O you who were to me even as a mother, O you who saved me from the river full of crocodiles, I cannot but suffer with you now in your suffering. But know this: everyone in the world who suffers is in harmony with the very secret of life; for the secret of life is suffering, and suffering is hidden in all things. The Lord smote your son so that Pharaoh would acknowledge the might of the people of Israel, and it is for this that Pharaoh will let the Lord's people go. And it is for this also, that another son, who is waited for, may one day be born into the world.

'Certain it is that, in the scales of life and death, only the Eternal Lord knows the weight of souls. Yet understand this, the great truth among all truths: it is out of sorrow that the worlds have been built; and at the birth of a child, or of a people, or of a star, there is always pain.'

And with an aspect of sorrow and profound resignation, Pharaoh called Moses and Aaron unto him and said, 'Rise up, and get you forth from among my people, both you and the children of Israel, together with your oxen and your ewes.'

And Moses and Aaron went away in silence, and nothing remained in that place save a man and a woman who were crying, just as, on that same night, so many fathers and mothers cried.

Two Ghosts on the Nile

It is well known that, during the last years of his life, Oscar Wilde was treated as the 'pariah dog of the nineteenth century'. The occasions on which he was able to forget his sufferings have been less well chronicled. After his incarceration, Wilde could not bear to be alone; between the cloister and the café, he chose the café. And there, in what he referred to as 'the ninth circle of the boulevards', he was, on occasion, able to 'talk of purple things and drink of purple wine' just as he had done before his trials. As a result, many wonderful tales and fragments of tales survive from this period.

Many of Wilde's listeners wrote his stories down in some detail. Others, however, were only able to recall their titles or their outlines. One woman, for example, remembered a story about a nurse who kills the man that she is nursing; another friend recalled a story entitled 'The Problem and the Lunatic', but was unable to recollect the plot. The following tale is typical of many of the extant fragments of Wilde's spoken stories in so far as only the paradoxical ending has survived.

RECLINING ON OPPOSITE BANKS of the River Nile, two ghosts, one of a man and the other of a woman who had in their lives both been Saints, told each other the story of their days among the living.

And, at the end of their long conversation, after the ghost of the man had uttered the dolorous tale of his life – a life of complete renunciation and sacrifice, a life that had been crowned with the glory of martyrdom – he made conclusion and said, 'And this body to which I denied all the joys of nature, this body that I mortified and which the whips have lashed, this wretched body that my torturers have burnt and destroyed, this vile carcass that has always been to me as an enemy – do you know what they did? After my death, they embalmed it with perfumes and spices!'

The Holy Courtesan

Oscar Wilde wrote down a large part of the following story as a play over the Christmas period of 1893 in a black book he kept in his bedroom at Tite Street. The return of Lord Alfred Douglas from Egypt early the following year apparently distracted him from the task of completing the play; he was, he said, unable ever to take it up again as the mood in which it had been conceived had passed.

However, in the following two years, Wilde frequently told the story of the play, which he called *La Sainte Courtesane*, with characteristic enthusiasm; he also referred to the unfinished play on a number of occasions. 'Yes,' he replied to a friend who asked how the play was progressing, '[The Courtesan] still continues to say wonderful things, but the anchorite always remains mute. I admit her words are quite unanswerable. I think I shall have to indicate his replies by stars or asterisks.' Later, in prison, he remarked to the same friend, '[The Courtesan] no longer says marvellous things, the robbers have buried her white body and carried away her jewels…'

On his release from prison, Wilde told the tale many times, sometimes giving it the English title 'The Holy Woman', sometimes referring to it as 'The Woman Covered with Jewels'. On occasion, he also expressed the desire to complete the dramatic version of the story that had been left unfinished. To encourage him to do so, his friends returned to Wilde the black book that contained parts of the play. But, having received the manuscript of a play he had once called a 'beautiful, coloured, musical thing', Wilde promptly left it in a cab. A few days later he laughed about the loss: a cab, he said, was the proper place for it. As a result, he never completed his play, and Robert Ross was able to publish only a fragment of a first draft in his collected edition of Wilde's works.

The following version of 'The Holy Courtesan' was told as a story to Robert Hichens some time in 1894. Hichens's version of the story is certainly not the most 'poetical' to have survived, but it is included here, along with Hichens's accompanying observations and Wilde's ongoing commentary (in italics), as it vividly evokes the image of Wilde in the act of narrating. It also captures something of Wilde's attitude to his own inventions: they were works in progress that went on developing in ways that he could neither predict nor control.

ONCE THERE WAS A MONK who lived alone in the Thebaïd and a famous courtesan who practised her profession in Alexandria. The monk was a rigid ascetic and had a holy horror of sin. The courtesan held all virtue in contempt, thought chastity (especially in a man) ridiculous, and lived entirely for the senses, for passion, for luxury and for reckless pleasure.

Rumour, busy even in the desert, brought to the monk tidings of this beautiful and terrible woman, of her power over man and the destructive force she exercised for the sole pleasure of doing evil. In faraway Alexandria, tidings of the monk also reached the ears of the courtesan, and roused at first her contempt, then her curiosity, and finally a desire to turn him from his ridiculous virtue and his emasculate holiness to the knowledge and practice of those bodily pleasures she knew so well how to arouse and to drive on into passion and frenzy.

In the desert, the monk said to himself, 'I will make a pilgrimage to the great city, and there I will turn this woman from her wickedness, subdue her, convert her, and force her by my virtue to throw herself at my feet for the glory of God.'

In Alexandria, the courtesan said to herself, 'There is no man born of woman who can resist me when I put forth my power. I will go to the desert and show the world how easy it is for a beautiful woman to turn a saint into a sinner. The monk shall become my lover.'

Now a woman who has made up her mind to do something is

quicker to act than a man who has made up his. And so it was that just as the monk was about to set out on his journey to Alexandria, the courtesan appeared before the door of his miserable dwelling and demanded admittance.

The monk came out, and there, in the sand of desolation, a debate took place between the lean, fierce and fervid ascetic and the voluptuous temptress…

Wilde then sketched this debate for me in a few characteristic words, uttered with his usual nonchalance, as of a man carelessly dropping treasures by the wayside.

Each of the antagonists was obstinate and, in consequence, the debate was long and, ultimately, indecisive. It ended thus: when the monk told the courtesan to return to Alexandria and change her life of sin for a life of holiness, she contemptuously rejected his proposal. Then the monk disappeared into his hut and the woman was left outside the closed door.

Here Wilde paused, and presently I said, 'Is that the end? Is that all?'

Oscar Wilde put up his hand to his mouth, in a gesture very characteristic of him when he was preparing a coup. It did not entirely conceal the smile that was curving his lips.

'No. What happened was this.'

In the debate which had seemed to lead nowhere, both the monk and the courtesan had, in fact, converted the other. And as the courtesan struck on the door to tell the monk she would turn her back on a life that had now become hateful to her, the monk opened it and came out crying, 'Take me with you to Alexandria. I have not lived. I have never known life. Teach me to live – with you!'

'And then?'

'Then, then,' he waved the hand which he had lifted to his mouth, 'I suppose they changed places. She remained in the desert, and he set out alone for the distant city. I have not worked all that out. My point is that the sinner had converted the saint and that in the same debate about good and evil the saint had converted the sinner. That's rather nice, I think. And it might have happened. Everything happens.'

Wilde in Naples, 1897. He is reported to have said, 'How I should love to be a troubadour... telling romantic stories to while away the tedium of the lives of the great.'

The True History of
Androcles and the Lion

During his final years in Paris, one of Wilde's greatest pleasures was to meet old friends. Those who had the courage to ask him to dine with them soon discovered that he could be as brilliant as ever. One friend whom he saw regularly was Lord Alfred Douglas. Whenever Douglas was in good spirits, he met Wilde at the Café de la Paix or at the Café Julien in the late morning, then took him out to a lunch at Maire's restaurant.

At Maire's, Wilde narrated stories that were so light and so witty that Douglas compared his words to the play of sunlight in a fountain. Characteristically, Wilde followed these with fables and biblical stories, which he narrated with a voice that trembled with emotion. 'The luncheon at Maire's lasted from twelve-thirty to five-fifteen,' wrote Wilde of one such occasion. 'Bosie had vine leaves in his hair and saw the moon at midday.'

During these meals, Douglas heard hundreds of Wilde's stories: fairy tales, anecdotes and the plots of many unwritten plays; the phrase 'I have thought of a story' was, he later recalled, forever on Wilde's lips. It should hardly surprise us, then, that in the *Sonnet* Douglas wrote after Wilde's death, what he laments most is the loss of so many marvellous tales. He evokes the image of Wilde the storyteller conjuring 'wonder out of emptiness' and mourns the loss of 'Forgotten tales and mysteries half said'.

Douglas was able to recall the outline of 'The True History of Androcles and the Lion', which has been conflated here with another extant version of the tale. Wilde may have told this other version to a dentist in Paris while he was waiting to have a tooth filled with gold.

T HOUGH NONE OF THE AUTHORITIES take the trouble to allude to the matter, it is well known that the slave Androcles was the most remarkable dentist of his day. Indeed, so great was his reputation that the Emperor of Rome himself asked Androcles to accompany him as the imperial dentist when he embarked on his expedition to Africa.

One day, on the edge of a vast desert, Androcles came upon a lion that appeared to be in a great deal of pain. The lion had, it seems, been foolish enough to attempt to eat the tough flesh of an Anglo-Saxon who had come to colonize that part of Africa. The poor beast had, in consequence, broken all of his teeth.

When Androcles heard his groans, he took pity on the lion and decided to give him a perfect set of golden teeth absolutely free of charge. When Androcles had performed the delicate operation, the lion thanked him profusely and ran off into the desert.

Now, some years later, during the time of the first persecution, Androcles, who was a very good Christian, was denounced and taken to the Circus of Rome. There, along with his fellow believers, he was thrown to a pack of hungry lions in front of all the nobility of Rome and his former master, the Emperor. As Androcles stood in the middle of the Circus, a lion bounded out of his golden cage and headed straight towards him with his mouth wide open.

Now, when Androcles looked inside the mouth of the lion he recognized the golden teeth he had put there so many years before, and the cry of fear that had started to come from his lips turned into a cry of joy. And the lion, realizing that it was his old friend the dentist, laid down meekly before him and licked his feet.

While he was licking the feet of Androcles, the lion started to wonder how he could best show his gratitude to the man who had once treated him free of charge. Then, after a while, the lion thought of a wonderful way to give the dentist great publicity in front of the Emperor and all of the Roman nobility. And so, rising up on his hind legs and letting out a loud roar, he devoured Androcles in a few mouthfuls, in order to demonstrate the excellence of the golden teeth which the dentist had made.

The Cardinal of Avignon

According to some commentators, the idea for a play called 'The Cardinal of Avignon' came to Wilde in America during his lecture tour of 1882. He wrote down the following outline of the play in 1894, probably at the request of a theatre manager or an actor who wanted to produce it.

Robert Ross later remarked of the play, 'I scarcely think [the manuscript] ever existed, though Wilde used to recite proposed passages from it.' As we have seen, this was entirely characteristic of Wilde. Although no account of him in the act of describing this particular play seems to have survived, one such occasion is preserved for us in the memoirs of a man who attended a meeting between Wilde and several theatre producers. Wilde had promised to deliver to them the completed four acts of yet another projected work, the society drama *Mr. and Mrs. Daventry*.

On arriving an hour late at the Café de la Paix, Wilde announced to the company, 'Gentlemen, I have here with me one of the four acts of the play that I promised to deliver to you finished today. Certain things have occurred which have made it impossible for me to write down the remaining acts, but they are all here [at this point Wilde tapped his forehead, then sank into the chair facing them and lit a cigarette], only you must give me wine – yellow sparkling wine – and plenty of it. Then I will tell you the play, and I will write down the last three acts tomorrow.'

Champagne was ordered for Wilde and, as he drank it, he described the play with such brilliance and in such detail that the men imagined that they were attending its first performance. He made ingenious suggestions concerning the acting, the scenery and even the audience; he also quoted long extracts from the dialogue and effortlessly conjured up all the characters with a few sentences. He went on in this way for over an hour and a half, then, promising them that he would write the play out by the end of the week, he stood up to take his leave.

His listeners were so impressed by his outline that they gave him a great deal of extra money on account. Wilde bowed to them with a flourish, refused to shake their outstretched hands and then plunged into the stream of passers-by on the avenue de L'Opéra, never to be seen again by any of them.

Wilde is reported to have told the outline of 'The Cardinal of Avignon' to a number of people during his final years in Paris; sometimes he narrated it as a story, on other occasions he described it as though he were watching a performance of it from the stalls. The 1894 scenario of the play, rather than one of the versions that Wilde narrated as a story, is reproduced here, as it allows us to imagine him in the act of describing the play to a group of friends or prospective backers.

THE PLAY OPENS IN THE PALACE of the Cardinal at Avignon. The Cardinal is alone and somewhat excited for he has received news that the Pope is sick and about to die. 'What if they were to elect me Pope?' he says to himself.

Some Nobles and Princes enter; and the Cardinal, who knows the vices and pleasures of each one, solicits and obtains pledges of their votes by promising each of them the fulfilment of their personal aims and desires. They leave and the Cardinal says: 'Will God place me on such a pinnacle?' – and he has a fine speech with regard to the Papacy.

A servant then enters and says that a young girl wishes to see the Cardinal. He refuses, but the beautiful young girl, who is the Cardinal's ward, enters of her own accord. She upbraids him for refusing to see her, and a very pretty and affectionate conversation occurs between them.

In the course of the conversation the girl says, 'You have spoken to me of many things, but there is one thing you never told me about, and that is Love.' 'And do you know what Love is?' the Cardinal asks her. 'Yes,' she replies, 'for I am in love.'

Then she explains to the Cardinal that she intends to marry a handsome young man who, for some time, has been a member of his Court and who has been made much of by him. The Cardinal is suddenly upset and makes her promise not to mention their conversation to her lover.

When his ward has left him, the Cardinal is filled with rage and sorrow. 'And so my sin of twenty years ago has risen up against me,' he exclaims 'and come to rob me of the only thing I love!' For the young man is his son.

The scene now changes to the gardens at the rear of the Palace. The Cardinal's ward and her betrothed are together. They have a passionate love scene. The young man, mindful of what they both owe to the Cardinal, asks his love whether she has told the Cardinal of their betrothal. She, mindful of her promise to the Cardinal, says that she has not. He then urges her to do so as soon as possible.

At this point there enters a pageant, and suddenly a Masque of Death appears. This alarms the girl who sees in it a presage of some coming woe. But her lover dismisses the idea, saying: 'What have you and I, with our new-born love, to do with Death? Death is not for such as you and I.' The pageant then comes to an end, and the lovers part. The girl, in leaving, drops her glove.

The Cardinal comes out of the Palace, picks up the glove, and, at the same time, sees the young man. He is furious. 'So they have met!' he says. He is determined that he will not lose the only thing he loves, and so, in the course of the ensuing conversation, the Cardinal tells the young man, who desires to be told about his father, that, years ago, a mighty prince on his death-bed entrusted his two children to his care.

'Am I one of those children?' asks the young man, 'You are,' the Cardinal replies. 'Then I have a brother?' asks the young man. 'No,' the Cardinal says, 'but you do have a sister.' 'A sister! Where is she? Why do I not know her?' the young man enquires. 'You do know her,' the Cardinal answers. 'She is the girl to whom you are betrothed!'

The young man's heart is filled with horror and despair. The Cardinal then urges him to pluck this impossible love from his heart and also to kill it in the heart of the girl. The girl now re-enters, and the Cardinal explains that her lover finds that he has made a serious mistake and does not love her sufficiently to wed her.

After some time the two lovers meet, and the young man carries out the promise exacted from him by the Cardinal.

The scene now changes back to the interior of the Palace, as at the opening of the play. The Cardinal is alone and is repenting of his deed of the previous day. He is miserable. A struggle goes on within him between his ambition and his love. He desperately loves his ward; but at the same time he doubts whether, with such a sin on his soul, God will raise him to the Papacy.

Trumpets are then heard. Nobles and Princes arrive. The Pope is dead, and the Cardinal has been elected Pope in his place. The Nobles and others leave after making obeisance to him.

The Cardinal is radiant. 'I who was but now in the mire am now placed so high, Christ's Vicar on earth!' And so on. A fine speech. Now his ambition conquers: he decides to allow his ward to marry the young man. He sends for the young man. 'What I told you yesterday was simply to test you. You and your betrothed are not related. Go, find her, and I will marry you tonight before I ride away to Rome.'

But at this moment the huge doors at the end of the hall are thrown open and friars enter bearing a bier covered with a pall, which they proceed to set down in the centre of the hall. They leave without speaking a word. Both men intuitively know who is on the bier. The young girl has killed herself in despair at the loss of her lover.

The Cardinal then opens the doors and says to the soldiers outside: 'Do not enter here, whatever you may hear, until I walk forth again'. He re-enters the room and draws a heavy bolt across the doors. The young man then says, 'Now I am going to kill you.' The Pope answers: 'I shall not defend myself, but I will plead with you.' And he urges upon the young man the sanctity of the Papal Office and represents to him the horrible sacrilege of such a murder. 'No,' he says, 'you cannot kill the Pope.' 'Such a crime,' replies the young man, 'has no horror for me: I shall kill you.'

The Pope then reveals to him that he is the young man's father, and places before him the hideousness of the crime of patricide. 'You cannot kill your father!' he says. 'Nothing in me responds to your appeal,' the young man replies, 'I have no filial feelings: I shall kill you.'

The Pope then goes to the bier and, drawing back the pall, confesses: 'I, too, loved her.' At this the young man runs and flings open the doors and says to the soldiers: 'His Holiness will ride hence tonight on his way to Rome.'

The Pope then stands, blessing the corpse, and as he does so, the young man throws himself on the bier and stabs himself. The soldiers, Nobles, Princes enter. And the Pope still stands blessing.

The Master

Towards the end of his life, Wilde would sometimes enjoy a nocturnal Paris that was 'lit up with beauty and with wine'. He and his friends gathered in the back room of a bar called the Kalisaya in the boulevard des Italiens. 'Kalisaya,' wrote Wilde, 'the American bar near the Crédit Lyonnais, is now the literary resort of myself and my friends: and we all gather there at five o'clock.'

While he drank gin or a cocktail of Champagne and whisky through a straw, Wilde would be presented to all the aspiring poets, anarchists and bohemians of Paris. In return for their homage and for the drinks they bought for him, he became 'rather wonderful' or 'quite amazing', in his own words, and charmed them with his stories. His performance went on for many hours; many of those who heard him remarked that he often talked better after an hour or so than he had done at the beginning.

On such occasions, Wilde retold and reinvented the tales published as *Poems in Prose*. One of these was probably 'The Master'. The fact that he continued to alter his works after they had been published suggests that Wilde did not regard them as 'definitive' simply because they had been written down. This fact also seems to contradict many traditional interpretations of Wilde's spoken stories, in which the tales are considered not as ends in themselves, but rather as 'preliminary experiments' he made before getting on with the more important business of writing.

This, quite clearly, was not the case.

WHEN JOSEPH OF ARIMATHEA came down in the evening from Mount Calvary, where Jesus had died, he saw seated on a white stone a young man who was weeping. And Joseph went near to him and said, 'I understand how great thy grief must be, for certainly that Man was a just Man.'

But the young man made answer, 'Oh, it is not for that I am weeping. I am weeping because I, too, have wrought miracles. I also have given sight to the blind; I have healed the palsied and I have raised the dead. I, too, have caused the barren fig tree to wither away and I have turned water into wine – and yet they have not crucified me.'

The Folly of Simon

The poet and journalist Ernest La Jeunesse heard many of Oscar Wilde's stories. Long after Wilde's death he would, like many of the storyteller's friends, mimic Wilde's voice and mannerisms as he retold them. In his evocative memoir of Wilde's final days, La Jeunesse recalled that, 'Slowly, word for word, Wilde would invent in his feverish, stumbling agony of art, curious and fleeting parables.'

La Jeunesse's memoir describes one of the very last occasions on which Wilde performed his tales. 'He attempts his stories all over again. It is nothing but the bitter, blinding brilliance of superhuman fireworks. All those who saw him at the close of his career, still spraying forth the splendour of his wit and invention, carving out the golden, jewelled fragments of his genius... will never forget the tremendous, tragic spectacle of one calmly damned yet proudly refusing to bend the neck.'

Because Wilde recast many of his old tales on these occasions, he may have retold the following story, which he had created in the early 1890s.

T HE OLD MAN SAT WITH HIS HEAD BOWED, as the recriminations of his angry wife rang in his ears.

'Senseless old fool! Why did you lose your time loitering on the way? Your father, and his father, and his father before him, were all keepers of the temple gate. And, had you been swifter when you were sent for, you would doubtless have been made keeper also. But now a readier man has been chosen in your place. Oh, most foolish old man who preferred to loiter on the way, so that you might carry the cross of some young carpenter, one who was in his life a seditious criminal!'

''Tis true,' said the old man. 'I met the young carpenter who was to be crucified and the centurion laid hold of me and bade me carry his cross. And after I had carried it to the top of the hill, I lingered on to listen to his words, for though he grieved sorely, his grief was not for himself, but for others, and the wonder of his words held me there, so that I forgot all other things.'

'Aye, truly,' his wife replied, 'you forgot all other things – and the little sense you ever had! And are you not ashamed to think that your father, and his father, and his father before him were all keepers of the gate of the Lord's house, and that their names are written upon it in letters of gold, which will be read by all men in the time to come? But you, vain old dotard, alone of all thy kin, will never be heard of again, for who in all the world, when thou art dead, will ever hear the name of Simon of Cyrene?'

The Useless Resurrection

In his last years, Oscar Wilde became a vagabond bard or troubadour. He journeyed through the boulevards of Paris and further afield to Italy and Switzerland, paying strangers for the drinks they bought him with the only currency he had left – his jokes and his tales. In the end, he talked to anyone who would listen: schoolteachers, journalists, students and young writers. One young writer who encountered him at this time recorded an extraordinary incident, which occurred during one of their meetings at the Café de la Paix.

While Wilde was narrating one of his tales, the young writer suddenly saw a resplendent golden angel coming towards their table from the middle of the Place de L'Opéra. The angel, which became bigger and bigger as it approached them on its feet of light, seemed to be holding an enormous lyre; noticing the startled look in the eyes of his listener, Wilde turned round in order to discover the cause. When he saw the angel he gasped and put his hand on the young writer's arm. Soon everyone in the café was looking at the angel; as they stood up many of them knocked over chairs and tables and some made the sign of the cross.

After a while, however, they realized that it was not the messenger from God come down to announce the end of the world, as they had imagined. Instead, it proved to be the projected image of a statue of Apollo on a nearby building, which had been refracted by the sun's rays and by the humid and dusty air of Paris.

Yet, even though the incident was explained away rationally, whenever the young writer happened to meet Wilde afterwards, he always 'saw' the golden angel with the lyre walking by his side. It is, of course, entirely appropriate that the image of the angel was a projection of a statue of Apollo, as many of Wilde's tales are a curious mixture of paganism and Christianity. The final tale, which follows here, is a classic example of a Christian story that has been developed in a pagan way.

Wilde first began to narrate the tale in the early 1890s; he appears also to have considered writing it down as a play. 'The Useless Resurrection' seems to differ from earlier versions of the story in so far as it concludes on a profoundly pessimistic note; others end with the acceptance of Christ's doctrine of joy and love throughout the world. Wilde apparently told it at the Bar Kalisaya on Christmas night in 1899, as a kind of 'refutation' of 'The Miracle of the Stigmata', the tale that had preceded it.

ONE DAY, AN ARAB LABOURER, employed by an archaeologist who was searching for ancient coins on Mount Calvary, by chance struck the stone of a sepulchre with his pickaxe. When, with the aid of his fellow labourers, he had lifted the heavy tombstone, he discovered a corpse still wrapped in an undamaged winding cloth inside.

On being informed of the macabre discovery, the archaeologist decided to remove it from the sepulchre and have it transported to a nearby museum. There, scientists wearing extraordinarily strong spectacles leaned over it and carefully unwrapped the winding cloth to reveal a mummified corpse inside. To their great astonishment, they discovered on the body wounds on the hands, on the side and on the feet. It was, beyond all shadow of a doubt, the body of Jesus Christ.

With this discovery it became quite obvious that generation after generation of believers had been deluded for two thousand years, from the holy women who first came to the tomb, to those whose knees had, over the centuries, worn away the stones of the sanctuary that was said to mark the exact site of the sepulchre.

Of course the newspapers of the world took control of the affair; they hounded the Pope out of Rome and caused their readers to turn away from the Christian faith. The Vatican itself was transformed into a temple dedicated to the god of Scientific Truth. And there, under glass, the corpse that had so sensationally destroyed two thousand years of belief was exhibited for the curiosity of the public.

But on the following Easter Sunday – a mournful Sunday on which no bells were rung to celebrate the glory of the risen Christ – a curious incident occurred.

When the first pale ray of the morning sun entered the room in the Vatican and touched the lifeless corpse, it suddenly rose up, smashed the windows of its glass prison and, before an astonished and prostrate public, soared in glorious flight out of the room.

Then an entirely new religion, based on individualism and joy and the worship of beauty, was created and spread throughout the world. There were new apostles and there were new martyrs, and, in certain places, the risen Christ appeared. He journeyed throughout the world in order to convince men of His existence, and to tell them of the new religion He had founded.

In a voice that was as musical as Apollo's lute, He announced to the world that all men who wished to lead perfect lives had to be completely and absolutely themselves. He declared that the imagination was the true basis of all spiritual life, and that the spiritual life alone was of any value. He preached a morality entirely based upon sympathy and he claimed that if men only believed in Him and followed his doctrine, there would no longer be any poverty or revolution or war in the world. There would be, He announced, a great harmony among the divided races and the divided classes, who would love one another and

Oscar Wilde in Rome, 1900.

come together to worship the permanent yet ephemeral miracle that is human life.

These, and many other things did Christ preach. For He had come back to bear on His shoulders the suffering of the entire world: those whose name is legion and whose dwelling is among tombs, oppressed nationalities, factory children, thieves, people in prison, outcasts, those who are dumb under oppression and whose silence is heard only by God.

His message to each and every man was simple: 'You have a wonderful personality. Develop it. Be yourself. For your perfection is inside of you.'

But, alas, Christ came too late into the world.

For this great miracle and this supreme revelation from the mouth of light were explained away rationally by the bespectacled scientists, and Jesus determined never again to reappear before the eyes of men.

And all things reverted to the apathy of the days before His appearance, days without either belief or Joy – dull, unimaginative days that had been but a mode of death.

Poems in Prose

*'Was this prose or was it poetry in a
new measure? A sense of his mastery of the
strange instrument held me in delight'*

SIX OF WILDE'S SPOKEN STORIES were written down as *Poems in Prose*, first published by Frank Harris in *The Fortnightly Review* in 1894. It is likely that two of them – 'The Disciple' and 'The House of Judgement' – were set down in order to please Lord Alfred Douglas, as they first appeared in the Oxford magazine, *The Spirit Lamp*, which Douglas edited. The other four – 'The Artist', 'The Doer of Good', 'The Master' and 'The Teacher of Wisdom' – were probably written at the request of Frank Harris, who included them, together with revised versions of 'The Disciple' and 'The House of Judgement', in *The Fortnightly Review*. As we have seen, Wilde told many fables and biblical stories at lunch parties given by Harris, and it is easy to imagine him writing them down soon after such an occasion. Since their appearance in *The Fortnightly Review*, the six stories have been republished many times in various editions of Wilde's works.

The *Poems in Prose* are republished here so that the reader may compare them with the versions Wilde narrated. Spoken versions of the prose poems can be found in this book under the titles 'The House of Judgement', 'The Man Who Could Only Think in Bronze', 'The Mirror of Narcissus', 'The Best Story in the World' and 'The Master'. No oral version of 'The Teacher of Wisdom' seems to have been written down.

A comparison of the prose poems with Wilde's oral versions allows us to understand the difference between his spoken and written styles. When he came to set down his spoken stories,

Wilde did so in a rather artificial and ornamental manner. Such a comparison also allows us to appreciate something of the universal disappointment of those who read the elaborate prose poems after having heard the author narrate them. Robert Ross, for example, wrote in his preface to *Poems in Prose*: 'To those who remember hearing them from Wilde's lips, there must always be a feeling of disappointment on reading them. He overloaded their ornament when he came to transcribe them, and some of his friends did not hesitate to make that criticism personally.'

Yet it was clearly Wilde's deliberate intention to write in a decorative way; he was writing according to the criteria of the specific genre of the 'prose poem'. This genre, developed in France during the eighteenth century, found its finest expression in the prose poetry of Stéphane Mallarmé and Charles Baudelaire. Irish and English writers, such as the poet Ernest Dowson, were greatly influenced by Baudelaire's *Petits Poèmes en Prose* (1869). Indeed, it is not unlikely that the style of Wilde's own contributions to the genre was inspired in part by Baudelaire's famous description of the ideal language of the prose poem. 'Who has not dreamed,' he wrote, 'of the miracle of a poetical prose, a musical prose without rhythm or rhyme?'

The following versions of *Poems in Prose* are taken from *The Fortnightly Review*. A relatively unknown version of 'The Disciple', published in *The Spirit Lamp* in 1893, has also been included.

The Artist

ONE EVENING THERE CAME INTO HIS SOUL the desire to fashion an image of *The Pleasure that abideth for a Moment*. And he went forth into the world to look for bronze. For he could only think in bronze.

But all the bronze of the whole world had disappeared, nor anywhere in the whole world was there any bronze to be found, save only the bronze of the image of *The Sorrow that endureth for Ever*.

Now this image he had himself, and with his own hands, fashioned, and had set it on the tomb of the one thing he had loved in life. On the tomb of the dead thing he had most loved had he set this image of his own fashioning, that it might serve as a sign of the love of man that dieth not, and a symbol of the sorrow of man that endureth for ever. And in the whole world there was no other bronze save the bronze of this image.

And he took the image he had fashioned, and set it in a great furnace, and gave it to the fire.

And out of the bronze of the image of *The Sorrow that endureth for Ever* he fashioned an image of *The Pleasure that abideth for a Moment*.

The Doer of Good

I T WAS NIGHT-TIME, and He was alone. And He saw afar off the walls of a round city, and went towards the city.

And when He came near, He heard within the city the tread of the feet of joy, and the laughter of the mouth of gladness and the loud noise of many lutes. And He knocked at the gate and certain of the gatekeepers opened to Him.

And He beheld a house that was of marble and had fair pillars of marble before it. The pillars were hung with garlands, and within and without there were torches of cedar. And He entered the house.

And when He had passed through the hall of chalcedony and the hall of jasper, and reached the long hall of feasting, He saw lying on a couch of sea-purple one whose hair was crowned with red roses and whose lips were red with wine.

And He went behind him and touched him on the shoulder and said to him, 'Why do you live like this?'

And the young man turned round and recognized Him, and made answer and said, 'But I was a leper once, and you healed me. How else should I live?'

And He passed out of the house and went again into the street.

And after a little while He saw one whose face and raiment were painted and whose feet were shod with pearls. And behind her came, slowly as a hunter, a young man who wore a cloak of two colours. Now the face of the woman was as the fair face of an idol, and the eyes of the young man were bright with lust.

And He followed swiftly and touched the hand of the young man, and said to him, 'Why do you look at this woman and in such wise?'

And the young man turned round and recognized Him, and said, 'But I was blind once, and you gave me sight. At what else should I look?'

And He ran forward and touched the painted raiment of the woman and said to her, 'Is there no other way in which to walk save the way of sin?'

And the woman turned round and recognized Him, and laughed and said, 'But you forgave me my sins, and the way is a pleasant way.'

And He passed out of the city.

And when He had passed out of the city He saw, seated by the roadside, a young man who was weeping.

And He went towards him and touched the long locks of his hair and said to him, 'Why are you weeping?'

And the young man looked up and recognized Him and made answer, 'But I was dead once, and you raised me from the dead. What else should I do but weep?'

The Disciple

WHEN NARCISSUS DIED, the pool of his pleasure changed from a cup of sweet waters into a cup of salt tears, and the Oreads came weeping through the woodland that they might sing to the pool and give it comfort.

And when they saw that the pool had changed from a cup of sweet waters into a cup of salt tears, they loosened the green tresses of their hair and cried into the pool and said, 'We do not wonder that you should mourn in this manner for Narcissus, so beautiful was he.'

'But was Narcissus beautiful?' said the pool.

'Who should know that better than you?' answered the Oreads. 'Us did he ever pass by, but you he sought for, and would lie on your banks and look down at you, and in the mirror of your waters he would mirror his own beauty.'

And the pool answered, 'But I loved Narcissus because, as he lay on my banks and looked down at me, in the mirror of his eyes I saw ever my own beauty mirrored.'

The Master

Now when the darkness came over the earth, Joseph of Arimathea, having lighted a torch of pine wood, passed down from the hill into the valley. For he had business in his own home.

And kneeling on the flint stones of the Valley of Desolation, he saw a young man who was naked and weeping. His hair was the colour of honey, and his body was as a white flower, but he had wounded his body with thorns and on his hair he had set ashes as a crown.

And he who had great possessions said to the young man who was naked and weeping, 'I do not wonder that your sorrow is so great, for surely He was a just man.'

And the young man answered, 'It is not for Him that I am weeping, but for myself. I, too, have changed water into wine, and I have healed the leper and given sight to the blind. I have walked upon the waters, and from the dwellers in the tombs I have cast out devils. I have fed the hungry in the desert where there was no food, and I have raised the dead from their narrow houses, and at my bidding, and before a great multitude of people, a barren fig-tree withered away. All things that this man has done I have also done. And yet they have not crucified me.'

The House of Judgement

A ND THERE WAS SILENCE in the House of Judgement, and the Man came naked before God.

And God opened the Book of the Life of the Man. And God said to the Man, 'Thy life hath been evil, and thou hast shown cruelty to those who were in need of succour, and to those who lacked help thou hast been bitter and hard of heart. The poor called to thee and thou didst not hearken, and thine ears were closed to the cry of My afflicted. The inheritance of the fatherless thou didst take unto thyself, and thou didst send the foxes into the vineyard of thy neighbour's field. Thou didst take the bread of the children and give it to the dogs to eat, and My lepers who lived in the marshes, and were at peace and praised Me, thou didst drive forth onto the highways, and on Mine earth out of which I made thee thou didst spill innocent blood.'

And the Man made answer and said, 'Even so did I.'

And again God opened the Book of the Life of the Man.

And God said to the Man, 'Thy life hath been evil, and the Beauty I have shown thou hast not sought for, and the Good I have hidden thou didst pass by. The walls of thy chamber were painted with images, and from the bed of thine abominations thou didst rise up to the sound of flutes. Thou didst build seven altars to the sins I have suffered, and didst eat of the thing that may not be eaten, and the purple of thy raiment was broidered with the three signs of shame. Thine idols were neither of gold nor of silver that endure, but of flesh that dieth. Thou didst stain their hair with perfumes, and put pomegranates in their hands. Thou didst stain their feet with saffron, and spread carpets before them. With antimony thou didst stain their eyelids and their bodies thou didst smear with myrrh. Thou didst bow thyself to the ground before them, and the thrones of thine idols were set in the sun. Thou didst show to the sun thy shame and to the moon thy madness.'

And the Man made answer and said, 'Even so did I.'

And a third time God opened the Book of the Life of the Man.

And God said to the Man, 'Evil hath been thy life, and with evil didst thou requite good, and with wrongdoing, kindness. The hands that fed thee thou didst wound, and the breasts that gave thee suck thou didst despise. He who came to thee with water went away thirsting, and the outlawed men who hid thee in their tents at night thou didst betray before dawn. Thine enemy who spared thee thou didst snare in an ambush, and the friend who walked with thee thou didst sell for a price, and to those who brought thee Love thou didst ever give Lust in thy turn.'

And the man made answer and said, 'Even so did I.'

And God closed the Book of the Life of the Man, and said, 'Surely I will send thee into Hell. Even into Hell will I send thee.'

And the Man cried out, 'Thou canst not.'

And God said to the Man, 'Wherefore can I not send thee to Hell, and for what reason?' 'Because in Hell have I always lived,' answered the Man.

And there was silence in the House of Judgement.

And after a space God spake, and said to the Man, 'Seeing that I may not send thee into Hell, surely I will send thee unto Heaven. Even unto Heaven will I send thee.'

And the Man cried out, 'Thou canst not.'

And God said to the Man, 'Wherefore can I not send thee unto Heaven, and for what reason?' 'Because never, and in no place, have I been able to imagine it,' answered the Man.

And there was silence in the House of Judgement.

The Teacher of Wisdom

FROM HIS CHILDHOOD he had been as one filled with the perfect knowledge of God, and even while he was yet but a lad, many of the saints, as well as certain holy women who dwelt in the free city of his birth, had been stirred to much wonder by the grave wisdom of his answers.

And when his parents had given him the robe and the ring of manhood, he kissed them, and left them and went out into the world, that he might speak to the world about God. For there were at that time many in the world who either knew not God at all, or had but an incomplete knowledge of Him, or worshipped the false gods who dwell in groves and have no care of their worshippers.

And he set his face to the sun and journeyed, walking without sandals as he had seen the saints walk, and carrying at his girdle a leathern wallet and a little water-bottle of burnt clay. And as he walked along the highway he was full of the joy that comes from the perfect knowledge of God, and he sang praises unto God without ceasing; and after a time he reached a strange land in which there were many cities.

And he passed through eleven cities. And some of these cities were in valleys, and others were by the banks of great rivers, and others were set on hills. And in each city he found a disciple who loved him and followed him, and a great multitude also of people followed him from each city, and the knowledge of God spread in the whole land. And many of the rulers were converted, and the priests of the temples in which there were idols found that half of their gain was gone, and when they beat upon their drums at noon none, or but a few, came with peacocks and with offerings of flesh, as had been the custom of the land before his coming.

Yet the more the people followed him, and the greater the number of his disciples, the greater became his sorrow. And he knew not why his sorrow was so great. For he spake ever about God, and out of the fullness of that perfect knowledge of God which God had Himself given to him.

And one evening he passed out of the eleventh city, which was a city of Armenia, and his disciples and a great crowd followed after him. And he went up on to a mountain and sat down on a rock that was on the mountain, and his disciples stood round him, and the multitude knelt in the valley. And he bowed his head on his hands and wept, and said to his Soul, 'Why is it that I am full of sorrow and fear, and that each of my disciples is an enemy that walks in the noonday?'

And his Soul answered him and said, 'God filled thee with the perfect knowledge of Himself, and thou hast given this knowledge away to others. The pearl of great price thou hast divided, and the vesture without seam thou hast parted asunder. He who giveth away wisdom robbeth himself. He is as one who giveth his treasure to a robber. Is not God wiser than thou art? Who art thou to give away the secret that God hath told thee? I was rich once, and thou hast made me poor. Once I saw God, and now thou hast hidden him from me.'

And he wept again, for he knew that his Soul spake truth to him, and that he had given to others the perfect knowledge of God, and that he was as one clinging to the skirts of God, and that his faith was leaving him by reason of the number of those who believed in him.

And he said to himself, 'I will talk no more about God. He who giveth away wisdom robbeth himself.'

And after the space of some hours his disciples came near to him and bowed themselves to the ground and said, 'Master, talk to us about God, for thou hast the perfect knowledge of God, and no man save thee hath this knowledge.' And he answered them and said, 'I will talk to you about all other things that are in heaven and on earth, but about God I will not talk to you. Neither now, nor at any time, will I talk to you about God.'

And they were wroth with him, and said to him, 'Thou hast led us into the desert that we might hearken to thee. Wilt thou send us away hungry, and the great multitude that thou hast made to follow thee?'

And he answered them and said, 'I will not talk to you about God.'

And the multitude murmured against him and said to him, 'Thou hast led us into the desert, and hast given us no food to eat. Talk to us about God and it will suffice us.' But he answered them not a word. For he knew that if he spake to them about God he would give away his treasure.

And his disciples went away sadly, and the multitude of people returned to their own homes. And many died on the way.

And when he was alone he rose up and set his face to the moon, and journeyed for seven moons, speaking to no man nor making any answer. And when the seventh moon had waned he reached that desert which is the desert of the Great River. And having found a cavern in which a centaur had once dwelt, he took it for his place of dwelling, and made himself a mat of reeds on which to lie, and became a hermit. And every hour the Hermit praised God that He had suffered him to keep some knowledge of Him and of His wonderful greatness.

Now, one evening, as the Hermit was seated before the cavern in which he had made his place of dwelling, he beheld a young man of evil and beautiful face who passed by in mean apparel and with empty hands. Every evening with empty hands the young man passed by, and every morning he returned with his hands full of purple and pearls. For he was a Robber and robbed the caravans of the merchants.

And the Hermit looked at him and pitied him. But he spake not a word. For he knew that he who speaks a word loses his faith.

And one morning, as the young man returned with his hands full of purple and pearls, he stopped and frowned and stamped his foot upon the sand, and said to the Hermit, 'Why do you look at me ever in this manner as I pass by? What is it that I see in your eyes? For no man has looked at me before in this manner. And the thing is a thorn and a trouble to me.'

And the Hermit answered him and said, 'What you see in my eyes is pity. Pity is what looks out at you from my eyes.'

And the young man laughed with scorn, and cried to the Hermit in a bitter voice, and said to him, 'I have purple and pearls in my hands, and you have but a mat of reeds on which to lie. What pity should you have for me? And for what reason have you this pity?'

'I have pity for you,' said the Hermit, 'because you have no knowledge of God.'

'Is this knowledge of God a precious thing?' asked the young man, and he came close to the mouth of the cavern.

'It is more precious than all the purple and pearls of the whole world,' answered the Hermit.

'And have you got it?' said the young Robber, and he came closer still.

'Once, indeed,' answered the Hermit, 'I possessed the perfect knowledge of God. But in my foolishness I parted with it, and divided it amongst others. Yet even now is such knowledge as remains to me more precious than purple or pearls.'

And when the young Robber heard this he threw away the purple and pearls that he was bearing in his hands, and drawing a sharp sword of curved steel he said to the Hermit, 'Give me, forthwith, this knowledge of God that you possess, or I will surely slay you. Wherefore should I not slay him who has a treasure greater than my treasure?'

And the Hermit spread out his arms and said, 'Were it not better for me to go unto the uttermost courts of God and praise Him, than to live in the world and have no knowledge of Him? Slay me if that be your desire, but I will not give away my knowledge of God.'

And the young Robber knelt down and besought him, but the Hermit would not talk to him about God, nor give him his treasure, and the young Robber rose up and said to the Hermit, 'Be it as you will. As for myself, I will go to the City of the Seven Sins, that is but three days' journey from this place, and for my purple they will give me pleasure, and for my pearls they will sell me joy.' And he took up the purple and the pearls and went swiftly away.

And the Hermit cried out and followed him and besought him. For the space of three days he followed the young Robber on the road and entreated him to return, nor to enter into the City of the Seven Sins.

And ever and anon the young Robber looked back at the Hermit and called to him, and said, 'Will you give me this knowledge of God which is more precious than purple and pearls? If you will give me that, I will not enter the city.' And ever did the Hermit answer, 'All things that I have, I will give thee, save that one thing only. For that thing it is not lawful for me to give away.'

And in the twilight of the third day they came nigh to the great scarlet gates of the City of the Seven Sins. And from the city there came the sound of much laughter. And the young Robber laughed in answer, and sought to knock at the gate. And as he did so the Hermit ran forward and caught him by the skirts of his raiment, and said to him, 'Stretch forth your hands, and set your arms around my neck, and put your ear close to my lips, and I will give you what remains to me of the knowledge of God.' And the young Robber stopped.

And when the Hermit had given away his knowledge of God he fell upon the ground and wept, and a great darkness hid him from the city and the young Robber, so that he saw them no more.

And as he lay there weeping he was aware of One who was standing beside him, and He who was standing beside him had feet of brass and hair like fine wool. And he raised up the Hermit, and said to him, 'Before this time thou hadst the perfect knowledge of God. Now thou shalt have the perfect love of God. Wherefore art thou weeping?'

And He kissed him.

The Disciple

WHEN NARCISSUS DIED the Trees and the Flowers desired to weep for him. And the Flowers said to the Trees, 'Let us go to the River and pray it to lend us of its waters, that we may make tears and weep and have our fill of sorrow.'

So the Trees and the Flowers went to the River, and the Trees called to the River and said, 'We pray thee to lend us of thy waters that we may make tears and weep and have our fill of sorrow.'

And the River answered, 'Surely ye may have of my waters as ye desire. But wherefore would ye turn my waters, which are waters of laughter, into waters that are waters of pain? And why do ye seek after sorrow?'

And the Flowers answered, 'We seek after sorrow because Narcissus is dead.'

And when the River heard that Narcissus was dead, it changed from a river of water into a river of tears.

And it cried out to the Trees and the Flowers and said, 'Though every drop of my waters is a tear, and I have changed from a river of water into a river of tears, and my waters that were waters of laughter are now waters of pain, yet can I not lend ye a tear, so loved I Narcissus.'

And the Trees and the Flowers were silent, and after a time, the Trees answered and said, 'We do not marvel that thou shouldst mourn for Narcissus in this manner, so beautiful was he.'

And the River said, 'But was Narcissus beautiful?'

And the Trees and the Flowers answered, 'Who should know that better than thou? Us did he ever pass by, but thee he sought for, and would lie on thy banks and look down at thee, and in the mirror of thy waters he would mirror his own beauty.'

And the River answered, 'But I loved Narcissus because, as he lay on my banks and looked down at me, in the mirror of his eyes I saw ever my own beauty mirrored. Therefore loved I Narcissus, and therefore must I weep and have my fill of sorrow, nor can I lend thee a tear.'

(From *The Spirit Lamp*, vol. IV, no. 2, 1893)

Note on the Translation and Editing

VIRTUALLY ALL THOSE WHO HEARD Oscar Wilde narrate his stories were disappointed when they read his 'prose poems'. In their view, Wilde had diminished the original charm and simplicity of the stories by using an over-elaborate and heavily 'jewelled' style. No doubt with this in mind, previous translators of the stories that survive in French have rendered them as simply and directly as possible.

Although some might argue that this restores freshness to the stories, it is impossible to imagine Wilde telling them in this way. From his letters and from every surviving report of his conversation, it is clear that he spoke with complex refrains and elaborate rhythmical phrases in the low, musical voice he gave to many of his own characters. Indeed, several listeners observed that Wilde told his stories as though they were a kind of word-music. One even compared him to a violinist who takes delight in emphasizing certain passages of music; another likened him to a bard who uttered magical words as though they were an incantation. If it is hard to imagine anyone speaking in this manner, we have only to recall the astonishment W. B. Yeats felt when he first met Wilde. 'I had never before,' he wrote, 'heard a man talking in perfect sentences, as if he had written them all overnight with labour and yet all spontaneous.'

Unlike previous translations, those included in *Table Talk* attempt to capture something of the voice with which Wilde told them. Although not as decorative as his *Poems in Prose* or the stories published in *A House of Pomegranates*, these renditions attempt to echo something of the author's less ornamental style. The translations of the anecdotes and comic tales have been inspired by stories such as 'The Canterville Ghost'; the fairy tales, fables and biblical tales are an imitation of Wilde's fairy stories and *De Profundis*.

While it is perhaps presumptuous to attempt to mimic Wilde's manner, it is nonetheless necessary if we are to imagine him in the act of telling the tales. It is, of course, impossible to reconstruct the authentic past in which these tales were told; Wilde himself teaches us that, whatever we imagine the past to have been like, our 'image' belongs very much to our time and to our own imaginations. But – as he also teaches us – this is beside the point: we can imagine how he might have told the stories and try to make our image as rich and as vital as possible. The prefaces are an attempt to evoke something of Wilde's presence; the translations are part of the same endeavour.

The translator of oral narratives is not constrained in the way translators of written literary works feel themselves to be. As the stories were written down by Wilde's listeners rather than by Wilde himself, there is no real point in translating them in a painstakingly 'faithful' or literal way. To do so would be entirely out of keeping with the spirit of Wilde's genius and with the spirit of the tales themselves; as one Wilde scholar has remarked, 'appropriateness' rather than strict 'authenticity' should be the aim. Accordingly, certain biblical formulae and one or two of Wilde's own rhetorical devices have been introduced into the translations.

It has also been deemed 'appropriate' to amend the spoken stories that were written down in English. Like every writer who has reproduced any of Wilde's spoken stories, the author of the current work has found it necessary to remove Victorian expressions, 'false notes' and certain infelicities of style. Five of the stories – 'The Actress', 'The Illusion of Free Will', 'The Rose of the Infanta', 'The Martyrdom of the Lovers' and 'The Shameful Death of Pope John XXII' – were evidently written down without a great deal of care; they are, in fact, so obviously inferior to the other stories that it has been necessary, in certain places, to rewrite them. 'The Story of the Man Who Sold His Soul', 'Jezebel' and 'The Face of the Soul' have, to a lesser extent, been altered for similar reasons. The sources for all of the stories can be found on pages 187 to 189.

Sources

ANECDOTES

'The Young Spendthrift': De Saix, Guillot, *Le Chant Du Cygne, Contes Parlés d'Oscar Wilde, Recueillis Et Rédigés Par Guillot De Saix*, pp 249-50, Paris, Mercure de France, 1942.

'Aunt Jane's Ball': Robertson, W. Graham, *Time Was*, pp 132-4, London, Hamish Hamilton, 1931.

'The Young Inventor': Shaw, George Bernard, 'My Memories of Oscar Wilde', in *Oscar Wilde*, by Frank Harris, Appendix A, pp 331-2, New York, Dorset Press, 1989 (reprint).

'The Actress': Enthoven, G. and (?) Lowther, *Son of Oscar Wilde* by Vyvyan Holland, Appendix C, pp 258-260, London, Hart-Davis, 1954.

'Presence of Mind': Pearson, Hesketh, *The Life of Oscar Wilde*, pp 211-2. London, Methuen & Co., 1946. Also Douglas, Lord Alfred, *Oscar Wilde and Myself*, pp 232-3, London, John Murray, 1914.

'Lord Arthur Savile and the Palmist': Pearson, pp 134-5.

'The Glass Eye': De Saix, pp 251-3.

'The True History of Anne of Cleves': Ricketts, C., *Recollections of Oscar Wilde*, p 17, London, Nonesuch Press, 1932.

'The Magic Ball', De Saix, pp 216-8.

FABLES

'The House of Judgement': Pearson, pp 218-9.

'The Illusion of Free Will': Le Galliene, Richard, *The Romantic '90s*, pp 146-7, London, G. P. Putnam & Son, 1926.

'The Rose of the Infanta': Sturge Moore, T & D.C. (eds.), *Works and Days from the Journal of Michael Field*, p 136, London, John Murray, 1933.

'The Face of the Soul': Hart-Davis, R., ed., *More Letters of Oscar Wilde*,
     Appendix B, pp 207-8, Oxford, OUP, 1985.

'The Poet': Ricketts, p 18.

'The Poet in Hell': Housman, L., *Echo De Paris*, pp 44-46, London,
     Jonathan Cape, 1923.

'The Counterfeit Coin': De Saix, pp 90-1.

Our Lady of Sorrows': Ricketts, pp 20-21.

'The Man Who Could Only Think in Bronze': De Saix, pp 284-5.

'The Story of the Man Who Sold His Soul': Housman, pp 47-51.

'The Mirror of Narcissus': Pearson, p 217.

Biblical Tales

'The Thirty Pieces of Silver': De Saix, p 104 and pp 286-7.

'The Martyrdom of the Lovers': Hamilton Graham, A., 'The Ephemeral',
     in *The Cornhill Magazine* LXXXI, December, pp 649-50, London, 1931.

'The Raising of Lazarus': From a letter of André Gide's, quoted in *Mercure de
     France* I XI, p 523, Paris, 1937.

'The Shameful Death of Pope John XXII': Hamilton Graham, pp 651-3.

'The Temptation of the Hermit': Conan Doyle, Sir Arthur, *Memoirs and
     Adventures*, pp 78-80, London, Hodder & Staughton, 1924.

'Salomé and the False Prophet': De Saix, pp 131-3.

'The Double Beheading': Ibid. pp 138-9.

'The Decapitation of Saint Salomé': Ibid. pp 135-6.

'Saint Robert of Phillimore': Leverson, Ada, *Letters to the Sphinx*, pp 48-9,
     London, Duckworth, 1930.

'The God Who Left his Temple': Ricketts, p 34.

'The Best Story in the World': Yeats, W.B., *Autobiographies*, p 286, London,
     Macmillan & Co., 1955.

The Exasperation of Nero: O'Sullivan, Vincent, Aspects of Wilde, p 67, London, Constable, 1936.

'Jezebel': Enthoven and (?) Lowther, Holland, Appendix C, pp 261-4.

'The Miracle of the Stigmata': De Saix, pp 126-7.

'Moses and Pharaoh': Ibid. pp 52-4.

'Two Ghosts on the Nile': Jaloux, E., Les Saisons Littéraires, Vol I, pp 170-1, Paris, 1942.

'The Holy Courtesan': Hichens, Robert, *Yesterday*, pp 68-9, London, Cassell & Co., 1947.

'The True History of Androcles and the Lion': De Saix, pp 140-1 and Douglas, p 232.

'The Cardinal of Avignon': Millard, C. S., 'Stuart Mason' in *The Bibliography of Oscar Wilde*, Appendix, pp 583-5, London, T. Werner Lowrie, 1914.

'The Master': Harris, p 80.

'The Folly of Simon': Enthoven and (?) Lowther, Holland, Appendix C, pp 260-1.

'The Useless Resurrection': De Saix, pp 170-2.

POEMS IN PROSE

'The Artist', 'The Doer of Good', 'The Disciple', 'The Master', 'The House of Judgement', 'The Teacher of Wisdom': *Complete Works of Oscar Wilde*, London, Collins, 1948.

'The Disciple': *The Spirit Lamp*, Vol 4, no. II, June 6, pp 50-1, Oxford, 1893.

Bibliography

The following works have been of great help during the
preparation of this volume:

Baudelaire, C, *The Poems in Prose*, trans. Francis Scarfe, London,
    Anvil Press, 1989.
Beckson, K. ed., Oscar Wilde: *The Critical Heritage*, London, Routledge &
    Kegan Paul, 1970.
Borges, Jorge Luis, *Selected Poems 1923-1967*, ed. N. Thomas Di Giovanni,
    London, Allen Lane, 1972.
De Saix, Guillot, *Contes et Propos d'Oscar Wilde*. Les Oeuvres Libres,
    Nouvelle Série, No. 40, Paris, 1949.
Ellmann, R. *Oscar Wilde*, London, Hamish Hamilton, 1987.
Gide, A. et al, *Recollections of Oscar Wilde*, Boston, J. W. Luce & Co.,1906.
Hart-Davis, R. ed., *The Letters of Oscar Wilde*, London, Hart-Davis,1962.
Kierkegaard, S, *Parables of Kierkegaard*, ed. T. C. Oden, Princeton,
    Princeton University Press, 1978.
Mikhail, E. H., *Oscar Wilde: An Annotated Bibliography of Criticism*, London,
    Macmillian, 1978.
Mikhail, E. H. ed., *Oscar Wilde: Interviews and Recollections*, 2 vols, London,
    Macmillan, 1979.
Murray, I. ed., *The Writings of Oscar Wilde*, Oxford, Oxford University
    Press, 1989.
Stokes, J., 'The Magic Ball' in *Oscar Wilde: Myths, Miracles and Imitations*,
    Cambridge, Cambridge University Press, 1996.
Toomey, D, 'The Story-Teller at Fault: Oscar Wilde and Irish Orality' in
    Wilde The Irishman, J. McCormack, ed., New Haven, Connecticut,
    Yale Univeristy Press, 1998.

Acknowledgements

I would like to thank the staff of the British Library and, in particular, that of Science 3 for their patient and efficient service. I would also like to express my gratitude to my agent Giles Gordon, my publisher Margaret Little, my editors Jamie Ambrose and Stephen Guise, to Susie Brumfitt, who typed out many of the stories for me, to Ingrid Cranfield, who copy-edited my 'prefaces' and to Anne Marie Wright for proof-reading the *Poems in Prose*. In addition, I would like to register a more private debt to Anna Wright and Dave Sprout for helping me with some of the titles of the stories, and to Peter Ackroyd for kindly agreeing to write the foreword. Most of all I would like to thank Chiara Nicolini, who, with great patience and intelligence, assisted me at every single stage of the writing of the book and, in particular, with the translations and the copy-editing.

Finally, I would like to thank Oscar Wilde's grandson, Mr Merlin Holland, for the interest that he has taken in *Table Talk* and for his kind permission to reproduce the spoken stories that are still in copyright. Although in the past Mr Holland has been reluctant to give his support to similar projects, he believes that, as there is now avid interest in every respect of Oscar Wilde's work and personality, an anthology of his grandfather's spoken stories will be welcomed by both scholars and general readers.

Picture credits

Hulton Getty 9; The Art Archive 16; Hulton Getty 27; Mary Evans Picture Library 30; Merlin Holland 34, 38, 50, 55; The Bridgeman Art Library /Stapleton Collection 62; Hulton Getty 67, 75, 86, 97, 105; Mary Evans Picture Library 111; Merlin Holland 123, 124, 133, 145; Hulton Getty 164.

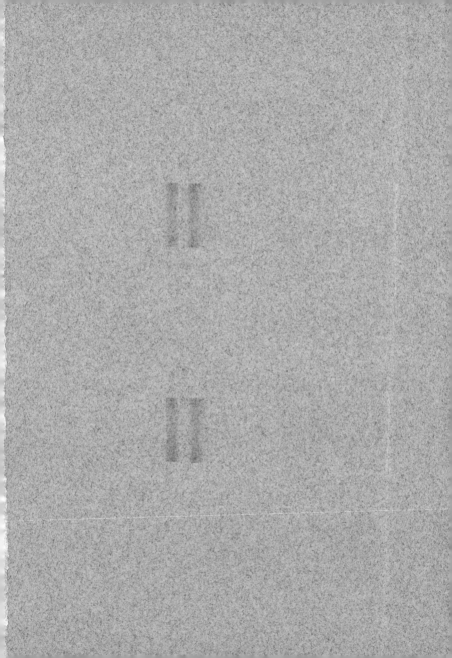